MILLER'S DAUGHTER

MILLER'S DAUGHTER

Nancy Potter

Illustrated by the author

'Once upon a time, when the birds ate lime
And the monkeys chewed tobacco,
A pig ran past with a feather in his arse
Crying, "What's the matter?" '

Larks Press

Published by the Larks Press
Ordnance Farmhouse
Guist Bottom, Dereham, Norfolk
NR20 5PF
Tel./Fax 01328 829207

October 1998

Printed by the Lanceni Press,
Garrood Drive, Fakenham

British Cataloguing-in-Publication Data
A catalogue record for this book is available from
the British Library

1

My father was a flour miller and corn merchant. The house in which I was born, in 1922, and in which we lived during my early childhood was part of the same building as the mill itself. The whole structure shook and rattled day and night, except, of course, for Sundays. The constant noise and vibration seemed most companionable to me, and I loved it, but Mother detested it. She longed to move to another house which would be quite separate from Father's business.

The Mill House was a part of the mill in every sense. The mill was Father's whole existence and it was natural and essential to him to live beside it so that he could feel the throb of its pulse twenty-four hours a day. As a move was impossible, indeed quite unthinkable for Father, Mother determined to make the best of things and to improve the Mill House. It was an ugly, square, red brick building with its frontage on one side of the mill yard, and there was plenty of scope for improvement. There was never a time when Mother and Father were not either planning, carrying out or paying for some alteration or redecoration scheme, and bickering over it. The house constantly rang to the sound of hammers and saws and workmen's footsteps. The mill carpenters and bricklayers had to do a lot of the work and were sent into the house whenever Father decided he could spare them from more pressing jobs. The mill men distempered the kitchen and pantry but a family firm of jobbing builders was employed as decorators in the rest of the house. We never seemed to have the place to ourselves for more than a few weeks after each alteration was finished before a fresh start was made and the men came trooping back again with ladders and wallpaper, pipes and fittings. Mother was forever instructing the daily woman and the maids how to clean up after the workmen. We children got our orders too. 'Come away from those ladders! Mind the paint! Don't touch that whitewash brush!' she told us. 'Mind the way!'

My sisters, Skinny and Millicent, were much older than I was and already going to school when I was born. I was, Mother told everyone proudly, her baby. This was a role she thrust upon me throughout my childhood and one which I was none too pleased to accept. Although Mother liked the romantic idea of a late baby, a child of her middle age, she had no intention of letting the reality of one check her plans for altering the house. By the time I was three years old she decided that the nursery was no longer necessary, and the wall between it and the dining room was pulled down to make the big room. Mother had always 'had a mind' for a big room. She went in for a dado, peacock blue wallpaper and a new red and blue carpet. Luckily she was forced to keep the beautiful old dining table of heavy oak, but she changed everything she could, and became more houseproud than ever as a result.

The big room was long and narrow. At one end a window looked out on to the mill yard and at the other French windows opened into the garden. They did not fit very well and in winter a terrible draught came through them. Father had sent his workmen to build a small wooden porch over the windows but it did not help the draught problem much and every autumn the mill carpenter had to come and nail boards over the worst cracks before the bad weather started. In the spring he came to open the windows up again.

It was quite a ritual. After he opened the windows it had to be summer, regardless of the weather. Mother liked 'everything nice'. We were allowed to go out through the French windows but not to come in again that way. 'Don't you come in here with your dirty feet again, dew I'll have your head off and a cabbage on!' she threatened. I never doubted that mother could do it and imagined us all walking about with cabbages instead of heads, so I did my best to remember never to run in that way from the garden

Our front door opened from the mill yard into a narrow hall-way with a black and white tiled floor. Sometimes the tiles seemed to make a pattern of diamonds, until I walked over them and they became squares.

On the opposite side of the hall from the big room were two smaller rooms, the drawing room and the wireless room. The wireless room had a door into the conservatory where my old pram stood at one end and at the other Father nursed his collection of orchids and ferns. Now and then he wandered about watering them and rearranging the pots. Mother grew a few plants in there too, and she liked to move Father's orchids away from the glass and put her own things in the best position. Then Father went in to examine his orchids and changed all the pots around again so as to improve the light for his favourites.

There was a constant battle going on over it as well as rows about watering, forgetting to water and watering too much, not to mention watering at the wrong time of day. To make this confusion worse, Skinny, who loved trying to grow plants and seeds, was determined to put some of her larger and better grown 'specimens' into the conservatory. She pushed them in between the other plants. There was a date palm and an orange tree which she had grown from pips. 'Who put them bloody things in there?' Father asked accusingly. He always blamed Mother. 'I haven't been in there, and I haven't touched your pots,' Mother replied. 'That isn't no good you mobbing me.' But whether Mother had done the mischief herself or allowed one of us to do it was of no consequence to Father. He said he 'didn't reckon that signified'. He always held Mother responsible for the behaviour of us children.

Leading out of the conservatory was a door into what had once been the old mill office until Father built a big new one on the other side of the yard. The room was in the mill itself and the machinery groaned and hummed overhead. It was supposed to be our play room although we seldom used it because it was cold and uninviting. There was dark patterned lino on the floor, two wooden arm chairs and an oak chest in which I kept my toys. The play room always seemed musty and there was a smell of meal coming through the narrow door which led directly into the mill. It was a trackway for mice going between the mill and the house, and we often saw them scamper across the floor. There were two large horrifying engravings on the walls. One showed the Charge of the Light Brigade, with horses dying in the foreground, their legs curled in final agony. The other depicted an election scene, with people fighting. The men were dying in that picture, and the fallen were being hit with sticks and election placards. I did not like playing in that room and preferred the wireless room. There I could stand at the round gate-legged table where we had tea in the winter time.

The wireless itself was a formidable horn contraption, standing on a cupboard which had been especially built by the mill carpenter to house its works. We children were never allowed to touch it and we were not permitted to speak while Father listened to the news. My father's big chair was in the wireless room and he went to sleep in it on Sunday afternoons and took a short nap there with his newspaper every

3

day after mid-day dinner. He came into the house promptly at one o'clock, shovelled his food down and retired to his chair to read and doze. Father's newspaper was sacred, and this was his first chance to read it as the papers were not delivered until noon. No one was allowed to open his paper except himself because he said 'women buggered it up'. They did not know how to handle a newspaper, he said, and there was a great fuss if anyone interfered with it so that Father had to rearrange the pages before he could begin to read. 'That's a masterpiece to me why you can't leave my bloody paper alone together, go to hell if that isn't!' he said, as he shook and pulled at it. Mother always had her own newspaper; it was the safest way. After reading for a few minutes Father lay back in his chair, put the newspaper over his face and composed himself for sleep. 'Wake me at two o'clock,' he commanded Mother, as she sat darning his socks. (The socks were of fine navy blue wool, and I felt they never really belonged to Father, they were not in character.) I do not know what came over Mother but one afternoon she just sat there and failed to wake Father at two o'clock. When Father opened his eyes and found that he had overslept he was furious. He refused to believe that Mother hadn't done it on purpose to rile him. He said he wouldn't put it past her. Although he was only a few minutes late he considered it a disaster and sprang out of his chair and dashed from the house and across the yard to the office, clapping his mill hat on his head as he went. He did not stop to swear at Mother that time.

The drawing room belonged to Mother exclusively. It had a sofa and two arm chairs with mauve chintz covers and pleated frills which hung down to the floor. I was forbidden to go into that room by myself for fear of what damage I might do. At one time there had been an ordinary window in the drawing room, overlooking the garden and the river, but Mother had 'had a mind' for a bay window, so Father had sent for the mill bricklayer who had contrived to build one for her. It made the room seem much larger and Mother was delighted with the result. She hung up mauve chintz window curtains, in triumph. The piano and also the gramophone were kept in the drawing room. We children were forbidden to touch the gramophone except under strict supervision. It was a vast mahogany cabinet on long legs and had compartments for storing the records on either side of the turntable.

You cranked it up with a handle, and if you wanted it to work you had to keep it cranked. The sound of those gramophones running down and being cranked up again is now, I suppose, lost for ever. Milly and I found it exquisitely funny, and if Mother did not stop us we let it run down again and again.

It was at the drawing room piano that Mother played hymns and my eldest sister, Skinny, thumped tunelessly. Milly and I were not considered musical enough to learn to play an instrument, so we were spared the agonies of practising, but we did have to listen to Skinny's efforts, and that was bad enough. Mother was a stickler for education, and she had made up her mind that Skinny was her musical daughter, so she responded to Skinny's disastrous piano playing by making her learn the violin as well. Skinny was very proud of her violin and when it arrived we each tried holding it with a cloth tucked under our chin to keep it steady. However even Mother had to concede that the noise Skinny made with it was painful. She was sent to practise it in the summer house where no one could hear her, and once there I suppose she practised less and less. Eventually no more was heard of the violin. Mother never mentioned it again. It was her rule never to admit that she had made a mistake, so in this case she just had to forget it.

The Mill House had a twisty front staircase, down which it was all too easy to fall. When she heard us running up and down in a hurry Mother would call out, 'Mind the stairs!' She did this quite automatically, scarcely lifting her head from the task she was engaged upon at the time, and equally automatically we ignored her words, and often came down head over heels as a result. There was no two-way switch for the landing light and we had to go upstairs in the dark and feel about when we got to the top before we could put the light on. Going round the staircase bend in the dark always frightened me. Mother made a great fuss when the stair carpet was taken up and put down again at spring cleaning, because it had to be folded very cunningly to fit round that bend. Nobody but herself ever did it properly, she said: they couldn't get it to go.

Upstairs the house was hideously inconvenient, with bedrooms opening out of one another. The culminating horror was the bath-bedroom which had to be crossed to reach the antiquated bathroom and lavatory. The bed in the bath-bedroom was never occupied if this could be avoided because it always resulted in a row. It was only used as last resort when visitors came to stay and the house was full of people. Father hated visitors as much as he hated the bath-bedroom, so when it was in use things were apt to become strained. At best Father was not a patient man and if, having got through the bath-bedroom, he found the bathroom occupied for too long, he simply broke the lock and burst in. The force of his entry landed him almost on top of anyone who happened to be sitting on the lavatory. I remember seeing him come crashing through the door. I sat there demurely waiting for him to retreat, secure in the knowledge that as I was on the lavatory, and not playing about, he was the one who was in the wrong. Right or wrong, it made him feel better to break something, and the mill carpenter always came along later to replace the lock. It never crossed Father's mind that this procedure might make him look foolish. If he had detected the slightest hint of ridicule on the part of the carpenter he would have sacked the man on the spot, so the carpenter kept his thoughts to himself and maintained a deadpan face, while every month or so he mended the door again. He had to be called in more often if Father was going through an extra touchy period, or Mother had too many relations staying in the house.

Milly and I shared a big bedroom, with blue paintwork, at the back of the house looking out over our very own small patch of garden and the river. The house stood at right angles to part of the mill, and from our bedroom window we could see into some of the mill windows. In the winter evenings we occasionally saw the millers passing as shadowy figures across the squares of light, and it was strangely comforting to know that the men were there, awake and working all night. One night I thought I saw the mill lights go out and I went and called Father. He was in bed, but got up and came in his bare feet and flannel nightshirt to stand at my window with me. The lights were showing again by then and everything looked normal, but he put on a coat and went across to the mill to make sure. I thought he might be angry with me for making a mistake, but next morning he said he was pleased I was keeping an eye on things.

Skinny had a small bedroom to herself because she was the eldest. The paintwork was pink and there was a huge pink built-in wardrobe cupboard. Skinny was fond of mice and she had repeatedly asked to

6

be allowed to keep white mice as pets, but Mother resolutely refused her requests. If Mother saw a mouse she used to jump on a chair and hold her skirts up above her knees while she screamed for someone to bring the cat. Plenty of mice strayed into the house from the mill. Occasionally, if the cat was not about, Skinny caught one herself, having cornered it behind a radiator. Then she held it up to show it to Mother, stroking it with her fingers and declaring she would keep it and tame it. This caused Mother's screams to be redoubled. She never felt she could trust Skinny over mice, and she began to suspect that Skinny was harbouring them in the bedroom cupboard. Mother' anxiety mounted until it overcame her reluctance. She armed herself with a crook-handled walking stick and, holding it at arm's length, proceeded to hook all Skinny's possessions out of the wardrobe on to the floor. She took Elizabeth, the white cat, into the bedroom with her, but no mice appeared. Elizabeth went to sleep on the bed, a forbidden pleasure, and Skinny had to clear up the mess. She bundled everything back without looking at it, effectively restoring the cupboard to its usual homely chaos.

As well as liking mice Skinny liked growing plants, and Mother encouraged this because it seemed harmless. There were germinating orange pips, lemons, date stones and seedlings of all kinds, which Skinny called her 'specimens' and which she kept in saucers all along the bedroom window sill and down behind the radiator, to keep them warm. I judged that Skinny's collection of 'specimens' was her dearest and proudest possession. One day, to retaliate for some insult or teasing, I went up to Skinny's bedroom and threw all her 'specimens' out of the window. I had quite forgotten that the porch, over the big room French windows, was directly below Skinny's bedroom window and I was astounded when I looked out and saw that all the seedlings had lodged on the porch roof instead of falling to the ground as I had expected. Skinny came and hung out of the window, crying with rage and frustration, but she failed to reach the 'specimens'. Both she and Mother believed that I had intended to get the seedlings stuck on the porch roof; they could not credit that I had simply not realised what would happen, and I was in disgrace. 'You shouldn't have meddled with them,' Mother said, and it was a long time before I was forgiven.

Every night Mother put my sisters' hair into curl rags. It did not do much for Milly, but Skinny's long dark hair hung in beautiful ringlets down her back. She was a very pretty child. The time came when Mother thought that Skinny was old enough to be trusted in the drawing room when ladies came to tea, so one day Mother called her in when she came home from school. Skinny, dressed in her navy blue gym slip and black woollen stockings, advanced into the room. She turned her large violet eyes on the assembled ladies. 'Did you know,' she asked them, 'that our well is full of corpse water?' The ladies looked at their tea cups in horror, and Skinny was hurried out of the room, while Mother hastened to explain that we never actually drank the well water. Every drop of drinking water had to be carried to our house. One of the men at the mill brought it from the nearby cottages, every morning and evening, in two huge white enamel buckets. Drinking water was precious, never to be wasted. As the house was so near the church the contents of the churchyard drained into our well, but we used that water for everything except cooking and drinking. No one suggested that we ought to avoid cleaning our teeth in the 'corpse water'. It had to be used all the time for baths, washing up, every other household purpose, and we all thrived on it.

The Mill House had a large square kitchen, with a black kitchen range and a small wall oven which baked bread beautifully. Mother kept the whole place scrubbed and cleaned nearly out of existence, and the maid had to blacklead the stove. The pantry, which opened out of the kitchen, was vast. In addition to providing shelf space for the buckets of drinking water, it also housed a large wooden 'safe' with perforated zinc front and sides to keep the flies off the food and, most important of all, an ice box which stood behind the door. Once a week the ice man came and carried in a mighty block of ice, wrapped in sacking so that he could keep a grip of it. 'Mind the way, the ice man is coming!' Mother called, as he staggered in manoeuvring his dripping load through difficult doorways. The block of ice fitted into the bottom of the ice box, and all the food which today would be stored in a refrigerator was piled above it. There were holes in the bottom of the box and a tray beneath to collect the water as it gradually dripped down from the melting ice. All this was quite normal. We had never lived in any other way, and no one in a country village expected mains water, drains or electricity. Our water closet upstairs was a precarious luxury,

8

and the privy in the garden was maintained as a second lavatory. The maids used it, and it was sometimes handy to have a downstairs lavatory which was easily accessible from the garden. We had electric light because it was 'made' in the mill, and carried into the house. Every Sunday when the mill was quiet someone had to go and start the dynamo to give us lights in the house before dusk. On winter afternoons it got dark while Father was still enjoying his after-dinner nap, and then Mother would go into the mill to start the engine. Father did not approve of her doing this so she lost no chance to demonstrate that she could do it to perfection. When she went across the yard to the mill on those shadowy afternoons she would almost run to get there before Father could wake and call her back. 'I suppose you couldn't wait a bloody minute till I woke up, could you?' he grumbled.

The first dog I remember in the house was Major, a liver-coloured spaniel, quite a big one. (Mother always called him a 'spanel'.) He used to come to the French windows and ask to be let in, but Mother refused to allow him entry because his feet were dirty. I can remember Father finding himself in the same plight. He came in and out from the yard so many times one wet and muddy day that, after the daily woman had scrubbed the hall, Mother locked the front door. Unlike Major, Father did not stand there quietly and ask to be let in; he shouted and rattled the door, and finally burst in through the kitchen, just as Mother had decided to give way and had gone to unlock the front door. 'What the hell's going on?' he shouted. 'That's a bloody masterpiece, that is, when a man's locked out of his own house, go to hell if that isn't!' Mother did not lock him out again, but following that outburst of fury, prolonged for several days, she explained to us, 'Your father may use a few swear words, but I've never heard him have any low talk, I will say that for him.'

Father was not fond of animals and he did not hold with keeping pets. 'I had a belly full of animals time Grand-dad was alive,' he said. Father's father, also a miller, had looked upon his son as a convenient form of slave labour and had made him milk the cow and see to the pony before going on the early milling shift, so poor Father had been forced to rise at four o'clock every morning and work until night. Grand-dad liked dogs and during the period of Father's apprenticeship he bought a new one and tied it up to the kennel in the yard. 'That bugger barked all bloody night,' Father told us, 'so I said I'd go down and give it a good thrashing, but Grand-dad said I wasn't to touch it. "Do you let that be," he said. "That isn't doing no harm," but that kept me awake night after night and come the end of the week I'd had about enough. I went down and tied a couple of bricks round the bugger's neck and slung it in the river. When morning come Grand-dad said, "Where's my dog?" and I said, "I've drowned the bugger." He never said no more. He knew he was in the wrong, and he couldn't expect me to work all hours if I didn't get no rest of a night.'

Although Father never got fond of a dog he saw the need to keep a good terrier for ratting. He thought all animals should earn their keep, and he saw to it that his did so. There was a succession of dogs which were chained up to the kennel behind the mill and only let loose to work. They were all Prince or Peggy. Father was always coming home with a fresh dog; he never bought puppies. I do not know why his dog turnover was so rapid; I never asked. One time, after Major had disappeared, presumed dead, Father bought a big Airedale terrier bitch, and as usual brought his latest purchase straight into the house to show Mother. Directly she came into the room the Airedale went straight to Mother and lay down at her feet. Mother said she would call it Sally. The dog was not meant for the house any more than all her predecessors had been, but somehow she wormed her way in. That dog loved Mother. Although it was a good ratter, to Father's amazement it clearly preferred being in the house with Mother to going ratting with him. If Mother went out of one room into another Sally got up and followed her. One evening Mother was up and down a lot, going backwards and forwards to see to things in the kitchen. Every time she went the dog went too. Last of all Father lost patience. 'Why the hell can't you sit down, you uneasy old bitch?' he demanded, flinging aside his newspaper. Mother whirled round in the doorway. 'What's that I heard you say?' she asked him, and Father had a job to convince her that he had been talking to the dog. Father was reluctant to let Sally prefer Mother, but he could not hold out against the two of them. It was not long before Mother was saying, 'Where's my Sally?' if Father took the dog out, so he had to give in and get a second dog for himself.

There were always too many cats. They went slinking across the mill yard, weaving between the sheds and buildings, flitting about their

business, stopping occasionally to sit and sun themselves on the brick wall over the river. They were of every size and colour but none of them were fat. Black and white predominated, although there was the odd one or two with tortoiseshell markings, and several scrawny tabby ones, which we called 'Old Cyprus'. One of the Cyprus had no tail at all and was known as Mankey. They were all supposed to be working cats to keep down the rats and mice in the mill. Father forbade Mother to feed them, but she could not resist doing so. 'I told you not to feed them cats,' Father exploded. 'You can't leave nothing alone; you aren't never satisfied without you're stuffing the buggers both ends!' Mother used to wait until Father had gone out in his car and then she nipped across the yard with an enamel pan of bread and milk which she put down behind the nearest door of the mill. 'Puss, puss, puss, teet, teet, teet,' she called, and from all over the buildings cats came running. The cats liked being fed and they came to the door of the house to ask for more. They sat on the step and howled. "The poor things are hungry,' Mother said. When Father came home and found the cats on the doorstep he aimed a few angry kicks at them and they scattered like

11

shadows, running back to the mill. 'What do you want to kick them poor cats for?' Mother asked in outrage. 'They haven't done anything to you.' Although Father did not like cats he still appreciated the importance of a good working animal. When the millers found a litter of kittens they were expected to tell Father. He would not allow the men to disturb them. I was always taken to see the kittens, curled warm against their mother on a dry nest of sacks in some remote and carefully chosen corner of the mill. 'Do you leave the cat alone,' Father told his millers. 'That'll hunt to feed the kittens.'

Indoors mother had Elizabeth, a beautiful fluffy white cat, with odd eyes. She populated the whole district. White kittens were in demand and she liked to try to have her litters in Mother's bed. Mother used to chase upstairs and bring her down whenever she saw Elizabeth making for the bedroom, but as soon as the coast was clear the cat would sneak up again; she sat at the foot of the stairs, lashing her tail with indignation, waiting for Mother's back to be turned so that there was a chance to make another dash for the bedroom. So determined was Elizabeth that she once tried to climb a ladder, left by the painters, to get into an upstairs window. She fell when she got half-way up, and we saw her hurtle past the window of the big room, where we were having dinner. She did not seem any the worse for this adventure but we all got very worked up about it. Mother kept saying, 'Poor Elizabeth, poor Elizabeth!' but Father said, 'Bloody old cat!'

The Mill House was a wonderful place for children. If the weather was wet, or I was confined indoors with a cold or getting over measles, I could look out into the yard, and there was always something to watch. Lorries and carts were continually coming and going. Almost all the men employed by Father lived in the village and went home to dinner at midday, but carters coming to the mill from elsewhere, to deliver or collect loads, had to bring their dinners with them. They had bread and cheese and a bottle of cold tea each, and they sat in the sun with their backs to the creeper-covered wall of the blacksmith's shop, cutting up lumps of bread and cheese and putting it into their mouths with their shut-knives. I used to practise doing this on the quiet. Mother was horrified when she saw me. She said it was a low way to eat, I was sure to cut my mouth, and I was never to do it again. All the workmen who came to the house and were given cups of tea drank from the saucers, never out of the cups. I watched them carefully so that later on I could try to copy them. It required a steady hand and the nerve to risk getting caught by Mother, but nevertheless I had a go at it.

There was a big garden behind the Mill House, and when she was not occupied in altering the house Mother like to think up schemes for improving the flower garden. She 'had a mind' for a rock garden which was not an easy wish to gratify. In East Anglia we hardly knew what a rock looked like. We were accustomed to see pieces of flint and stones scattered about the fields, and flint in old buildings and walls, but rocks did not come into our daily lives at all. Father had to get a load of rocks sent from foreign parts just to please Mother. One of the mill men came during the summer evenings to build them into a rock garden. When it was finished Mother was delighted and immediately wanted a lily pond full of goldfish to go in the middle of the rocks. She wanted it just a few yards from the river bank, never thinking for a moment that it might look odd there. As soon as the mill bricklayer had constructed the pond in a careful circular design, she 'had a mind' for a fountain to go in the middle of that. From somewhere she acquired a little stone boy who held a stone water bottle, out of which the river water was going to pour into the lily pond. When the statue arrived the elderly and highly respectable bricklayer was thankful to see that Mother had chosen a modest little boy. 'We didn't want nothing rude ma'am,' he told Mother as he cemented the fountain in position.

The river ran all down one side of our garden, under the mill and away to the town. There was a little wooden gate in the brick wall which bordered the river, and steps led down from the gate to boats which were tied up there. We were forbidden to open the gate or use the boats unless one of the parents was with us. Pink rambler roses grew all along the wall and hung down into the water, their reflections swaying tranquilly as the river slid by beneath them. In winter the garden was often flooded, sometimes to quite a depth, and I once had the pleasure of watching Milly try to walk through the floods on stilts and fall into the water. Floods were a regular occurrence, quite normal in our part of East Anglia. Sometimes the water was high enough to prevent us getting to school or, having got there, the flood level would rise behind us so that Mother had to send a frantic message to the school telling us to start home immediately or risk getting cut off and having to stay there all night. The school strongly disapproved of these alarms and I had great difficulty in convincing my teacher that I was not making up an excuse to get home early.

Father saw floods as a necessary evil and, apart from having the wheat shed floor raised above any likely flood level, he ignored them. He liked to start up the mill on the water turbine on Monday mornings and he held up a good head of water over the weekend for that purpose, sometimes flooding the upstream marshes in the process. The more determined farmers who grazed those marshes occasionally dared to protest. A small boy, one of the farmer's sons, would arrive on his bicycle on Sunday afternoon with a message. 'Our marsh is now flooding. My dad say, please will you lift the sluice?' 'Oh ah!' was all Father said when Mother relayed the message to him, after the cyclist had gone. Father maintained that if the buggers didn't like what he did they could bloody well lump it. Mother had to set about trying to talk him round; she did not want him to upset the people in the village. Sometimes she succeeded and Father agreed to go and raise the sluice gate an inch or two, but only if it was nice weather for a walk along the river bank. He never went if it was raining. Various local authorities and individuals tried from time to time to get Father to co-operate in having something done about the floods. The river was several feet higher than the surrounding water meadows and marshes. If we stood in the meadow behind our garden the top of the river bank was well above our heads. When the banks gave way in times of flood, matters were serious and the local farmers were fearful for the fate of their livestock. This did not concern Father. 'Let them grumble,' he said. 'I haven't never seen a poor farmer yet.' In the end a Catchment Board was set up to try to control the flooding, and Father joined it. He knew from the start that it was doomed to failure, but he liked being on the Board so that he could keep telling everyone else how foolishly things were being done, in spite of his good advice, freely given. He scorned the whole enterprise. 'The water would soon get away,' he explained, 'if them lot of duzzy fools would stop trying to hold it back.' This was unanswerable, as of course the floods always went down after a day or two, but by that time the damage had been done.

Mother liked reading aloud to me from what she called 'nice

educational books'. One of her favourite stories was about the little Dutch boy who spent all night with his hand in a hole in the river wall to prevent the water breaking through and flooding the surrounding district. 'He lay there all night,' Mother said, 'until help came; he was a hero.' It always amazed me that Mother was taken in by this tale. I felt sure that Father would have seen through it immediately. How could that boy have been a hero? He was just another 'duzzy fool' trying to hold back the water.

A huge yew hedge marked the boundary of our garden on the side opposite the river. Next to the yew hedge we had a tennis court. We lost hundreds of balls in that hedge and it made Milly savage. She used to beg Father to have the court netted, but he said it was a 'lot of squit' and flatly refused to do so. We spent hours searching the thick yew for lost tennis balls, and rarely found them unless they had gone right through into the 'deek' the other side. The 'deek' was on Father's property, as was the narrow footpath which ran along between it and the churchyard wall. The 'deek' drained into a culvert below the mill roadway and past the lorry sheds, to join the main river. It was a good place for frog's spawn and frowned on by Mother. Nevertheless Mother herself found the 'deek' useful when she suddenly 'had a mind' for a rustic bridge. Father decided to make one for her over the 'deek' beside the mill roadway and got his carpenter to construct it with a rustic hand rail either side. He even planted a weeping willow by the bridge, and Mother was delighted with the whole effect. She never saw that it looked a little out of place.

The church was so near us that it almost overshadowed the house. The graveyard bounded our land on two sides for, as well as having its wall running parallel with the yew hedge and 'deek', the churchyard extended all down one side of the mill roadway. The flint wall was high on our side, which made it difficult to climb, but we often managed it, getting a precarious foothold between the stones and hoisting ourselves up, although this was strictly forbidden by Mother. Inside the church-yard the level of the ground was about four feet above our roadway, so it was easy to jump down and pick the luscious blackberries which grew there. Mother said we were not to eat them. They were not very nice, she said, because they had been nourished by the corpses. She always found a reason to stop us doing what we liked, and declared

15

blackberries picked by the roadside to be 'not nice' because of the dust. Whenever possible we paid no attention to her instructions. Ours was a very old churchyard and the graves were piled high on top of one another. On summer evenings it was sometimes possible to see mauve phosphorescent lights glowing and dancing above the graves. It was an eerie but a fascinating sight. We were none of us afraid of the graveyard; we were too familiar with it for that. From our garden we could hear people singing in church, and if we made much noise they could hear us. On Sunday evenings in summer Mother spent a lot of time telling us not to 'shriek in the garden'. On Sunday mornings she was in church herself and usually took my sisters with her. I had to go too, as soon as I was judged to be old enough to sit still.

II

Mother said that Sunday was supposed to be a day of rest and she thought it would be nice to stay in bed a little longer on Sunday mornings, but Father utterly refused to do so. All the week he was up early enough to have his breakfast and get across to the office by eight o'clock, when work started there. He saw no need to change his breakfast time on Sundays. 'If you got to bed good time of a night,' he told us, 'you wouldn't want to lay-a-bed of a morning.' Bed was one of the things Father nagged about. Generally he left all the routine things in our upbringing to Mother, and held her responsible for it, but when it came to going to bed he felt strongly enough to tackle us himself. After we had gone to bed he liked to sit in the wireless room and read in peace, and he got furiously angry if he could hear us running about and laughing overhead. He would come out into the hall and call up the stairs, 'Now then, together, don't you let me hear another dean!' which quietened us immediately.

On Sundays we had clean underclothes, tickly woollen vests which were torture, and long woollen stockings, difficult to pull on. Everyone wore best clothes on Sundays, or at least not their every-day ones, and certainly their best for going to church. Father wore his second-best grey suit. He always had grey suits and grey hats so that they would not show the flour dust from the mill; that is, except for his funeral clothes which, of course, were black. He wore cream-and-blue-striped flannel shirts in winter and fine silky blue poplin ones in summer, and he always had starched white collars fixed on with studs, and much swearing. Father's ties were narrow hand-knitted silk ones, in rather careful dark colours. When she was first married Mother used to knit his ties herself, but the arrival of babies put a stop to such leisurely activities and Father had to get on as best he could with bought ties of a similar kind. The knitted silk was springy and easy to tie, and he would never have considered wearing anything else. Father had well-polished black lace-up boots of soft leather. He never bought brown ones and he never bought a pair of shoes in his life. He expected all his clothes to be very neat, and Mother had to keep them carefully mended and supplied with buttons. Ignoring fashion, Father did not wear a chain on his big gold pocket watch, because he thought it might dangle about and get in his way. Instead the watch was attached to his waistcoat button by a flat little leather strap, which kept it safe should it fall out of his pocket. Upstairs in his bedroom he had a magnificent silver watch which, as well as telling the time, showed the phases of the moon and stars. He always kept it beside his bed and let me see it sometimes as a special treat. It was a remarkable and lovely thing to possess, and Father treasured it.

Mother told us that when she and Father were first married he had been most unwilling to have a lot of clean clothes, but she had persuaded him by saying, 'A man in your position would expect to have a clean collar every day.' Father had thought deeply about this and, never one to reject a good idea, regardless of its source, he decided to follow Mother's advice. Thereafter, in matters of dress, Father felt his social position keenly and was determined to be seen to be correct. He did not buy new clothes often, but he always bought good quality things. Sometimes he got a shock when the bills came in. 'I aren't having no more of that,' he said. 'That's highway robbery. I'd rather black my bum and go naked.' Father's mill hat and his everyday going-out hat, both grey, hung side by side in the hall. The mill one had a fine coating of white dust and sweat had seeped through the band to stain the ribbon. Otherwise the hats were exactly alike. Father's best hat was the same grey again, but he kept it upstairs. When the mill hat got too bad to wear it went to the jumble sale, and he down-graded the other hats and bought a new one, just like the rest, to keep in his wardrobe. One day he went into Lacton wearing his mill hat, having forgotten to change it before starting out. When he discovered what he had done he swore at Mother for not noticing, and failing to tell him before it was too late. The smell of Father was a blend of whisky, strong pipe tobacco and thick clothes not often cleaned. I complained to Mother and said I was never going to get married because I did not like the smell of men. 'Oh, that's only old men what smell like that,' she told me, reassuringly. 'Young men smell all right.'

Father never made any concession to a heat wave other than to take his jacket off in the garden and exchange his grey hat for a panama. He always wore braces, never a belt; he was not really the right shape for a belt. His face and hands used to get sunburnt, but never his arms, which were creamy white, like his neck below the collar line. Although he was dark-haired, grey when I knew him, and hazel-eyed, his skin was exceptionally pale. He was long-nosed and narrow-jawed, with teeth all pushed together, crossing one another in the front. He had one or two false teeth on a plate which he made a great deal of fuss about. The plate was left in the bathroom overnight, and someone was usually on the lavatory with the door locked when Father's teeth were required for breakfast. If it was one of us in the bathroom Father had no problems or inhibitions about bursting in, but a visitor could really hold him up, and he raged about outside the bathroom door shouting, 'That bugger's in there and I can't get my bloody teeth!' Mother tried to quieten him, but not before a horrified dressing-gowned figure had dashed out and run for cover, so that Father could snatch up his teeth and clatter downstairs to breakfast.

Sundays demanded a big hot midday dinner, more elaborate than the hot weekday dinners we usually had, and Mother bustled round getting ready for church and seeing to the cooking at the same time. My sisters went to church, but I was left at home with Father when I was little. Those Sunday mornings with him were some of the best times I ever had, yet I never remember protesting at giving them up to go to church when Mother decided I was old enough for it. It was what happened when you were older, and seemed inevitable. In any case I expect Father had had enough of entertaining me by that time and was not sorry to see me go off with the others.

When the mid-morning church-going party left, Father and I set off to have what he called 'a walk round'. We went round the mill and all the buildings and often inspected the apple trees, of which Father grew a great number. He used to show me how to prune the trees and graft them. He said I had green fingers, and if he had a special tree to graft he made me do it, and sure enough it always proved successful. Almost all the trees produced cooking apples. The bulk of the crop went to market, but to make use of the surplus or damaged fruit Father had started a small cider press. He kept it in a dark shed next to the blacksmith's shop, and the smell from it was fearful. If you made cider, Father explained, naturally you had to keep tasting it, to see if it was coming along satisfactorily. He often tasted his latest brew, sometimes with the help of one or two friends. A collection of dirty tumblers was

kept in the shed and used again and again. His guests were not fussy, and after the first tumblerful of Father's cider they could scarcely keep their feet, let alone criticise the glasses. That cider was enough to knock out most people, but not Father; his whisky drinking had all but immunised him to the effects of alcohol, and he got great amuse-ment out of watching the unwary drinkers who expected cider to be harmless.

On many a Sunday morning we took the terrier and went after rats. Father carried his gun and took shots at any rats the dog put out. I was instructed to hold the back of Father's coat and never to leave go. I carried out this order faithfully, hanging on for dear life, sometimes having to run to keep up with him, or sidestep smartly to avoid being swept off my feet. Once I let go, and Father swore at me. He was really angry, and I never did it again. Whilst he felt me dragging along behind him he knew could shoot in safety and not hit me, and could give all his attention to the dog and the rats. We had some fine chases. I saw a rat try to swim the river, but the terrier plunged in after it and killed it in mid-stream.

As well as having a Sunday morning walk round, Father was partial to inspecting his property before he went to bed. Almost every evening, winter and summer, he would put on his old coat, take his gun, and go to let the dog loose. If he saw a rat he shot it, and the dog was encouraged to run in and out between the banked-up corn sacks and around all the sheds and outbuildings, looking for rats. What with the corn stock, the pig food and the chickens, not to mention the flour milling process itself, rats were a real problem and they had to be checked constantly.

One winter evening soon after Father had gone out with Prince, the kitchen door opened again. Father was standing on the step. 'I've shot my dog!' he said. Mother looked up from what she was doing. 'What do you mean, you've shot your dog?' she asked. 'What I say,' he told her desperately. 'I've shot my dog!' Pale as a ghost Father leaned against the door post. 'I'll have to get the car out and get him to the vet,' he said. 'That's the first time I ever had a black dog, and blast, I couldn't see that was him, and I shot him. That's a good little old dog,' he said. 'I wouldn't have done that for worlds.' He propped the gun up in the corner behind the kitchen door and hurried off. Father reckoned Prince was the best ratter he ever had. Certainly he was the oddest-looking dog which ever passed through Father's hands. He was small, with a little pointed face and narrow, delicate legs and feet. His coat was a dusty brownish-black, smooth on the head and back but with curly feathers down the backs of his legs and on his chest. His bushy tail curled wildly, and his eyes were steady black beads. He never got excited, and was to be trusted in the most awkward situations; above all he was a deadly killer. Father really valued him, and fortunately the shot did not prove fatal. Prince recovered and came home, after his stay in the vet's kennels, apparently as good as new. He still carried his tail in its crazy curl over his back, and he still enjoyed going ratting with Father for several more years. One day he disappeared and was never seen again. Father could not get to the bottom of it, but he declared that Prince must have been stolen because he was such a good ratter.

My Sunday expeditions with Father were often enlivened by the company of Bob. He was the mill blacksmith and engineer, a lovely ageless person with twinkling blue eyes and a deeply cleft chin. He

21

had dark hair in the dent in his chin, where he could not shave, and a liberal pasting of engine oil lodged there too. The blacksmith's shop was Bob's place. He worked in it all the week in an atmosphere of grease and iron filings. It was dark and dank, but Bob was boss in there and no one else was allowed to touch his tools without his permission. When he emerged from this den it was either to tend the big engine which produced the power to run the mill, or to give advice on some machine or contrivance which was being troublesome.

On Sunday mornings Bob came ratting with us in his working clothes, and the smell of them was the same as the smell of the blacksmith's shop. He wore navy bib-and-brace overalls stained black with grease, and carried his folding two-foot rule stuck in the top pocket. Under the bib and brace were his collarless flannel shirt, waistcoat and trousers. Over the top went a shapeless old blue jacket, the pockets bulging and sagging with nails and screws, nuts, pencils and twine. His heavy boots, once black, were a dusty mauvish-grey, the round toes protruding from under the wrinkled legs of his overalls. He was never seen without a cloth cap on his head, and although his working cap was rather greasy it still lent dignity to his appearance. Bob's movements were unhurried, but he got through an immense amount of work and was greatly respected by everyone at the mill. He was the most calm person I ever knew, and I never remember Father losing his temper with him. 'He daren't start on Bob,' Mother said. 'He knows he couldn't run the mill without him.' Bob was a great help when he came ratting with us. He armed himself with a long iron stake which he poked down the rat holes, and he could always suggest a good place to find a rat. Sometimes we met Bob out walking on Sunday afternoons, and then he was hardly recognisable as the person I knew. He had a clean tweed cap on his head and wore a brown suit with a gold watch-chain across the waistcoat. Stout Mrs Bob, dressed in her best hat, walked primly beside him. Only the twinkle in his eye remained unchanged, and I could still see the dark stain in the cleft of his chin.

Some Sunday mornings were even more enjoyable than the ratting ones. There was watercress to be gathered by the sluice, and Father was very fond of watercress. It was a long walk over the fen to the sluice gates, and we had to cross three little plank bridges which only had handrails at one side. 'You keep hold of the rail,' Father cautioned me. 'I don't want to see you duzzy in.' The planks were slippery with green slime from the dripping willow trees in summer, and white with frost in winter, so it was wise to heed his warning. We used to see all manner of birds when we crossed the fen. 'There go Jack Snipe!' Father exclaimed, as a little greyish pointed bird darted away, almost from under my feet. We saw kingfishers on the fen, and once there was a bird which Father guessed was an avocet. The fen was a lovely, watery, windswept place, just for us and a few grazing cattle. In winter perhaps there would be no more than a couple of horses standing silhouetted against the flat landscape, their manes and tails streaming in the wind.

One Sunday when Father and I went to pick watercress, I fell in. Father was angry, because he had told me to keep to the edge of the stream where the water was shallow, while he waded into the middle. It seemed to me that the best cress grew in mid-stream and, throwing caution to the winds, I stepped forward to follow Father and sank up to my waist in the muddy water. Father dragged me on to the bank and emptied the water out of my boots. 'What the hell made you do that?' he asked. 'I told you to stop where that wasn't deep; you want to mind what I say, my lady.' It was a cold day, so Father had to abandon his watercressing and hurry me home. Although it was a long walk I was still soaked when we got back to the house. Father took me upstairs and sat me on the bathroom chair while he peeled off my wet brown woollen stockings. I just stayed there, waiting for him to find some dry clothes for me, but this he completely failed to do. He got more and more irritated as he searched. I could not tell him where my clean clothes were kept, and he could not believe that I was such a fool as to be unable to help him. Father swore. It seemed vital to get me dressed in dry things before Mother got home from church and made a fuss, but he did not manage to do it. As soon as she got back to the house Mother came upstairs, and when she heard that I had fallen in the water she was very cross indeed. 'You didn't ought to have let her do any such thing,' she told Father. 'She'll catch her death.'

Autumn brought a Sunday when the hazel nuts were ripe. Then Bob carried a short wooden ladder and set it up against the summer house so that we could get up on to the flat roof to harvest them. We

23

picked great basketfuls. Bob climbed the tree to get the nuts which we could not reach from the roof. Father and I agreed that he climbed as well as if he had been a monkey, but I was forbidden to make that comment in Bob's hearing because he might not think it sounded very nice. Nobody wanted to hurt his feelings, least of all Father.

On rainy Sunday mornings we sometimes did a bit of carpentry We did it in the carpenter's shop. It had a huge bench, and pieces of wood were stacked all round the walls. On the floor the shavings were piled so deep that I had to kick my way through them; they tickled my legs, and the smell of it was wonderful. Father was clever with his hands, and I was expected to be able to hold things correctly and to pass each tool as it was needed. When whatever Father was making proved too much for me to hold we had to change places. 'If I hold it,' he said, 'are you man enough to drive in the nails?' Father passed me the hammer. 'Only one woman in a hundred can drive a nail,' he said. Then it became a matter of pride for me to learn to drive nails in order to please him, and I hammered away with a will. Father had always wanted sons. He had intended to have sons and had made his wishes perfectly clear, but Mother had proved perverse. She produced three daughters. Things would have been different, Father declared, if he had had a boy. More than once he looked at me sadly as we worked in the carpenter's shop. 'You ought to have been a boy,' he said. 'I always wanted a boy. Every man wants a son, and I meant you to be a boy.' I do not know what a modern psychologist would have made of it, but Father's regrets, so freely expressed, never put me out at all. I knew he loved me, so it did not really matter that somehow things had gone wrong when I was born and that I was not the boy he had meant me to be.

Although Father was capable of doing most jobs around the house himself, he was seldom called upon to do so. The mill provided workmen to tackle almost anything which was needed, so it was only in the case of some evening or Sunday breakdown that Father had to set about doing the job himself. He made the maximum fuss and bother over it, fetching special tools from the carpenter's shop. Very often the breakdown was in the lighting system, and then I was required to hold the flashlight for Father to see what he was doing. I was expected to direct the beam of light in the best way for him to see his work, no matter how much he twisted and turned. If my concentration wavered and I failed to keep pace with his movements so that his hands cast a shadow on the work, he blamed me immediately. 'Why blast! Can't you even show a light properly?' he asked in disgust.

In the ordinary course of events Father never went to church. He said that religion was meant for women and fools. 'I reckon when the buggers just go and tell God what to do that's the time to pack up,' he declared. Funerals were the only church services he was willing to attend, as he considered them social necessities. When he got home from one he hurried upstairs to take off his funeral suit before sitting down to a meal at which he ate two helpings of every-thing to reassure himself that he was better off than the corpse. When he sat back satisfied, he told us, 'I'm going to be cremated. I don't want no one snotting and howling round my grave.' Father had never approved of religion. 'That fare to me that some bloody rum things went on in the Bible,' he said.

'King David and King Solomon led upright and godly lives
They were fond of goodly living and other people's wives,
But when old age o'ertook them and they were filled with qualms,
Solomon wrote the Proverbs and David wrote the Psalms.'

He chanted this verse to prove his point. Nevertheless Father was not above making use of the Lord's name if it served his purpose. When we children seemed to be lacking in determination Father expressed his scorn. 'Now then together, the Lord won't help them what don't help themselves,' he threatened. Father certainly helped himself; he had his way to make in the world and he got things done, but I doubt if he ever gave the Lord any credit for it.

After Sunday dinner Father had time for a longer and sounder sleep than he managed on weekdays. The noise of his snores was alarming. He used to read himself to sleep. He had all the Edgar Wallace books, Bulldog Drummond was a favourite, and also Rider Haggard's yarns. He had a complete collection of James Blyth's work, and he liked *Juicy Joe* above all. Mother disapproved of this light reading, and into the bargain she held that James Blyth wrote 'low old

25

books', but Father ignored her criticism and continued to enjoy a good read. When I was old enough to read myself I much preferred Father's books to those that Mother recommended, and I never touched my school compulsory holiday reading; I was always far too deep in the trash, as Mother called it. Because Father was asleep no one was allowed to make a noise on Sunday afternoons. If a favourite toy had been left in the wireless room where he slept, we just had to do without it until he got up. Sometimes I was bold enough to try to creep into the room to fetch what I wanted, but he was awake in an instant and started swearing. 'There isn't a mite of peace in this bloody house!' he yelled. Occasionally he would go back to sleep again, but more often he got up and raged about, finally banging out of the house to disappear for the evening. The only Sunday afternoons on which Father did not get any sleep were those summer ones when we all went to Gorleston. Character-istically he never gave Mother any warning. 'Do you want to go to "Golston"?' he would ask after dinner. 'Well then, look sharp and get your hats on.'

Holidays, that is to say traditional seaside holidays, for nothing more was ever considered, were a continual bone of contention for my parents. Father could never be away from home at harvest time because he was busy buying his wheat stocks for the coming winter. As this coincided with our school holidays, he never spent a complete holiday with us. Each year Mother took us girls to stay at Gorleston for a month and Father joined us at weekends. At first she hired a house, later tried boarding houses, and finally, when her youngest sister came to live there, used to borrow the Gorleston house while my aunt went to spend a month in Scotland with her in-laws. We always had a beach hut at Gorleston. It was painted up each spring and sent down to the beach on one of Father's lorries. It was a big white hut with double doors which hooked back, and shelves and pegs for bathing and picnic things. It had to be transported in pieces and assembled on arrival at the beach. I remember the fun of finding it on our first trip to Gorleston in the early summer. Our outings were always on Sundays, when Father could take us in the car. We never got far along the road before Father said, 'Have you got the hut key?' Then Mother would hunt through her bag, the bathing bags and the picnic basket. Sometimes the key was not there, and we had to go back to get it, amid fierce arguments as to whose fault it was.

When we stayed at Gorleston Father took us and all the luggage in the car and left us there. We did not see him again until the next Saturday. One fateful day, on arrival at Aunt's house I discovered that my teddy bear had been left behind. My tears flowed; I could not go to bed without my bear. Father promised that as soon as he got home that night he would find my bear and pack him up in a parcel. He said he would send the parcel to me on the lorry which was due to go through Gorleston to Great Yarmouth next morning. After Father left I kept worrying that he might forget my bear, but Mother assured me that he would not do so. Next morning, after a mournful and lonely night, I was playing in the little walled back garden when there was a sudden thump, and the sound of heavy footsteps going away. The lorry driver had thrown the big brown paper parcel which contained my bear over the high wall into our garden. I pounced on it. Father had not forgotten and I loved him for it.

The Gorleston holidays were splendid times. Mother liked the sea, so we all bathed, and I dug in the sand. Our enveloping bathing dresses came down almost to our knees. Mother had a black-and-white one, with a skirt discreetly over her thighs and white braid round the neck and sleeves. We used to keep a little methylated spirit stove in the hut and boil our kettle for tea. We had most of our meals there. The smell of meths still takes me straight back in my imagination to Gorleston beach. Having our own hut was very grand. Less fortunate people hired tents: these stood in row after row, dirty grey canvas flapping forlornly in the stiff breeze which seems never to stop blowing on the East Anglian coast. If people did not want to spend all day on the beach, but just came to have a bathe, they could hire one of the bathing machines. These were small, brightly-painted wooden huts on wheels. An enormous carthorse dragged them one by one to the water's edge as the tide receded, and dragged them back up the sand again when the tide came in, so that a person who wished to bathe could get straight out of the machine into the water. Ladies did not walk about the beach in their bathing dresses. To get from our hut to the sea Mother wore a brightly-coloured bathing wrap like a cloak, and all the other respectable ladies on Gorleston beach did the same.

When Father came at the weekend he always used to say, 'My

heart! You're all as brown as berries!' and he would say to Mother, 'Do you look at them girls!' He never paddled or bathed in the sea, but sat, black boots and all, in a deck chair by the water's edge, wearing his panama hat, while we came and went around him, wet and sandy as we were. Father made boats for me out of folded newspaper. They floated well until a wave capsized them. When a man came along the beach selling William pears from a basket, Father bought one each for us and halved them with his shut-knife, so that if we dropped a piece in the sand we did not lose the whole pear. Sometimes he peeled them too, turning the fruit deftly in his long brown fingers with the perfect filbert nails. It was a pleasure to watch.

Aunt's Gorleston house was one of a Victorian terrace, in a quiet tree-lined road, not far from the beach. At the front there were iron railings and a little gate opening on to a minute front garden, just a square of grass and a path to the front door. It was a very small house, and this in itself was a novelty to us, coming from the mill. The back garden was entirely enclosed by high brick walls. There were few flowers, but some sad evergreens and a patch of grass. A concrete path stretched from the back door to a gate in the far garden wall which opened on to the lane. This lane, not much more than a path between the garden walls, gave access to all the back gardens in the terrace. It was rather dark and smelly, and Mother discouraged us from using it. One of the things I liked best about Gorleston was the superabundance of snails in Aunt's garden. There seemed to be hundreds of them, and Milly and I collected them and organised snail races along the back garden path. Small active brown snails were the fastest. They could be persuaded to crawl in a more or less straight line by damping the concrete with a finger tip dipped in the rainwater butt. The snails nearly always kept to the wet finger lines. When we had chosen our snails we had to chant to them to gain their co-operation 'Hodderman, Dod-derman, put out your horns. The farmer is coming to cut your corns.' Then the snails were supposed to come right out of their shells and begin to crawl. The chant was magic and it did not have to make sense, but I knew that dodman was a Norfolk name for a snail. Mother had corns on her feet, and occasionally they had to be cut, so I supposed the snails had corns somewhere too. I did not ask any questions. All I required was a good supply of racing snails, and a bit of magic to help them along.

Early on weekday mornings a man used to come down our road selling bloaters. Mother went out of the house with a plate to buy some for breakfast. They were delicious. Another trader in that road was a man who cycled along with dozens of strings of onions dangling from his shoulders. Mother called him Johnny Onions, and told us that he was a Dutch man who had brought his produce over from Holland, away across the North Sea.

As Mother had lived at Great Yarmouth for a while when she was a girl, she knew the district well. On a rainy day when we could not go to the beach she took us on the paddle steamer up the river from Gorleston to Great Yarmouth. It was a lovely trip because there was so much to see. We went past the timber yards, piled high with golden-coloured wood, and past fishing boats moored to the quay, unloading their catch. When we got to Great Yarmouth we saw the Scottish fishergirls gutting the herring on the water front. The girls came down to stay in Yarmouth for the herring season, especially to do this work. They were highly skilled, and worked as fast as lightning. Most of the gutted fish were thrown into barrels of brine and sold as salted herring, while some were used for red herring, kippers, or bloaters. Bloaters were never salted, just smoked. The smell was fearful, but the girls, who were often young and pretty, did not seem to care. When they were waiting for the next catch to arrive they walked about Yarmouth knitting and laughing together. Many talked in Gaelic, and we could not under-stand a word they said. They were real foreigners, more foreign to us than Johnny Onions, because we never heard him speak. Watching the animated smiling faces of the fishergirls, I could not understand how they could look so happy, covered in fish scales as they were and stinking of raw fish so that one could smell it all the way across the quay.

Great Uncle Basil, Mother's uncle, lived near Gorleston, and he came to see us quite frequently while were staying in Aunt's house. He came in his pony trap and he left the pony, a staid old animal, hitched to a tree outside our front gate. It never showed any signs of restiveness, so perhaps it was glad to stand and wait for a while in the shade. Uncle Basil was a dear old man, with a flowing grey beard and a drooping moustache which got in his way when he drank his tea. The beard got in my way when I was asked to give him a kiss. I could never find a smooth part of his face to aim for, and my lips sank unwillingly into the wiry growth. He never failed to smile kindly at me, realising, no doubt, that the beard had made me a little afraid of him. Uncle invariably arrived when we were having breakfast. It probably seemed like the middle of the morning to him. He was a bachelor because, Mother said, he had promised great-grandmother that he would always look after his sister, Aunt Dolly, who was 'not quite right', so of course he could not leave her to get married. When I asked how she knew that Aunt Dolly was 'not quite right', Mother said that Aunt could not be trusted to get the dinner ready. When she made dumplings she made them all different sizes so that they never got cooked together in the same time. This showed beyond a doubt, Mother told me, that Aunt Dolly was 'not right' and could not be left to look after herself. Sometimes Uncle Basil brought his sister in the pony trap at breakfast time and left her to spend the day with us on the beach. She dressed entirely in black, including black boots and a black hat with a piece of elastic under her chin, like our school hats. Her chin was very bristly. I do not remember Aunt Dolly saying more than 'yes' or 'no' to Mother. She simply did not talk, but she was slow and gentle, and she never bothered anyone.

These Gorleston holidays were repeated year after year while I was a little girl, and eventually Mother began to rebel. She wanted to venture further afield and to persuade Father to go with her. The place she set her heart on visiting was Wales. Every time she mentioned the idea of a Welsh holiday Father said, 'I'm not going there; I might meet bloody old Lloyd George.' In the end Mother won, and they set off for Llandudno. Climbing into the train, strangely attired in new clothes, even a new hat, although still a grey one, Father remained adamant: 'If I see bloody old Lloyd George walking along the sea front, I'm coming home,' he said.

III

Aunt Eliza was Father's step-sister, and nearly twenty years older than he was. My paternal grandparents had a large family. Grand-dad had three sons and two daughters before his first wife died. When he married again he chose a widow, who already had one daughter, Aunt Eliza. Father was the only child of the second marriage, and Mother told us that he had been thoroughly spoilt. He was the delight of his parents' old age, and when Grand-dad died he left all his money and two flour mills to Father while, to their disgust, the older sons and daughters got nothing. Father was not popular with the other members of his family and, with the exception of Aunt Eliza, we hardly saw his relatives at all. There was Aunt Mary, who had chalk gout and liked to show her bad legs to Mother. She made quite a ceremony of rolling down her stout woollen stockings so that she could display her knees. Aunt Mary did not come to our house and, although Mother and I went to visit her occasionally, Father never did. There was an aged husband who ran a small business in a nearby market town, helped by their adopted daughter Alice. The daughter was very religious; she had been brought up strictly chapel, and she let it be known that the Lord had called her to missionary work in darkest Africa. Only the necessity to care for her adopted parents in their old age prevented her from answering the call. Everyone admired her, and for years she was considered a martyr by all the family, until eventually the old folk died. Alice inherited the business and the house, and we all waited to see her sell up and go to Africa. Instead of going, she enlarged and improved the business, and stayed on in the house, enjoying a very good income. Mother and Aunt Eliza decided that it seemed a very funny thing to them that the Lord's call could be so conveniently forgotten.

Father's third step-sister was Aunt Hettie. As a girl she had fallen in love and wished to marry, but Grand-dad did not approve of the proposed match and she was forbidden to see the man again. Obviously trouble was expected, because Grandmother locked Aunt Hettie in her bedroom to prevent her disobeying Grand-dad. Hettie was a spirited girl, and nimble too; she climbed out of the window in the night and eloped. She married the man of her choice and went with him to live in Australia, where she had ten children before he deserted her. She was forced to remain in a strange land and struggle to bring up her large family as best she could. No help came from Grand-dad. Because she had disobeyed him, Grand-dad never communicated with her again, and he decreed that in future her name was never to be mentioned by any of the family. Father was ready to comply with this. He thought Grand-dad was right, and that Aunt Hettie's husband's behaviour proved that Grand-dad's judgement had been correct. 'That wasn't as if she hadn't been warned,' he said. Father kept up this extraordinary feud for years, and Aunt Eliza appeared to do the same. She was totally dependent on Father, and could not afford to rile him, even if she had found the courage to stand up to him. It was not until years later, when Mother's globe-trotting took her to Australia for a holiday, that the matter was raised again. Mother told Father that she intended to meet Aunt Hettie in Australia. Father ignored this threat, as he did not believe that Mother could carry it out. Mother took pleasure in opposing Father whenever she could, and she got Aunt Hettie's address and went to see her. She must have got the information from Aunt Eliza, who had kept in touch with her half-sister for all those years, but she never told Father. Next time Aunt Hettie visited England she came to stay in our house, and there was not much Father could do about it, so the hatchet was finally buried, and brother and sister were reconciled at last.

The only one of Father's brothers whom I remember clearly was Uncle Ernest. He looked just like photographs of Grand-dad: broad-shouldered and thick-set, though not as tall as Father, he gave the impression of being almost square. He had a beard which prickled my face when he kissed me, but it was not so long or so rough as Great Uncle Basil's beard was. We were expected to kiss all our relations; it was the correct way to behave. Uncle Ernest was a widower with five grown-up sons, all flour millers. They provided the entire work force of his small mill, and Father envied him sorely. Mother maintained that his wife had died early because there was no plumbing in the house, and she had been forced to work too hard. 'That killed that poor woman, looking after all them men,' Mother said. After Uncle Ernest's wife had been dead several years Skinny and I went with Mother on a memorable visit to his house. The family lived in a bleak, dilapidated

mill house in West Suffolk, which reeked of damp and hopelessness. When we arrived all the menfolk were out at work, and we were greeted by the housekeeper, who had laid out a huge spread for tea. Uncle Ernest had told her to do that, and to invite us to begin the meal in his absence, as he expected to be late; but, for some reason best known to herself, Mother refused to let us do so. We peeped into the dining room and saw a table groaning under the weight of delicacies which, to our fury, we were not permitted to eat. Instead, the car came to collect us and Mother took us home without delay. The only thing she did allow us to do was to go to the privy before we left. We had to cross a damp meadow where the emerald green grass was cropped to a velvety smoothness by a menacing flock of geese. I eyed them warily, and tried to stop myself breaking into a run, which would have proved fatal as the grass was slippery with goose droppings. The privy stank. There was a bunch of newspaper squares, cut neatly and looped together on a string, suspended from a nail. Sitting there in the dim light which flickered through the small holes cut for that purpose in the top of the door, and which cast a strange pattern across my bare knees, I could understand that Uncle Ernest's wife might have preferred death. Mother herself refused to use the privy. 'I'm not going in there,' she said. 'That stink fit to putrefy a polecat,' and she held out until she got home.

Lacton Mill House was Aunt Eliza's home, as it had been Grand-dad's in his time. Father had been born and brought up there, and lived in that house until he married. Father told me wonderful tales about his childhood at Lacton Mill. He went ice-skating, fishing and rowing, always doing something on the river which ran past the garden of the house, and away under the mill. One of Father's older step-brothers kept a canoe on the river bank, and the day came when he decided to repaint it. Father and a friend of his, both weedy little boys, and always being teased and tormented by their elders, saw a good way to retaliate. They crept up behind the canoe owner whilst he was squatting down over his boat, paint brush in hand, concentrating on his work and, having armed themselves with two rotten eggs, they managed to place one under each of the bigger boy's heels. He was so absorbed in his task that he did not notice them, and Father and his friend crawled away to hide in the osiers and wait to see what would happen. Sure enough, when my uncle stood up he crushed the two eggs perfectly. Father said the smell was unbelievable. There was a lot of fun and mischief to get into around the mill, and the little boys made the most of it. It was no wonder that Father thought school a waste of time.

In Grand-dad's day Aunt Eliza had worked in Lacton Mill office, and she continued to do so throughout my childhood. The office had a big desk, at which she stood, under the window. I never saw her sit on the high stool. She had a gold fob watch hanging in a little fretwork frame on the far corner of the desk. There was a smell of meal and dust. Calendars for the previous ten years, with pictures painted by Milly and dutifully presented each Christmas, hung, one over another, from a nail on the wall, the backmost ones curling and yellow at the edges. The telephone was an ancient brass instrument, not often used. In the office, on a hook behind the door, Aunt Eliza kept the keys of the mill. They were attached to a very old marrow bone by a stout piece of twine. This had been Grand-dad's idea, so that if he lost the keys his bulldog could be sent to find them. Father said he could recollect the dog finding the bone with the keys on it and bringing it home, but refusing to give it up. Grand-dad hung the bone on its usual hook, with the bulldog suspended from it. 'That old dog hung there all day until his jaws got tired and he had to let go,' Father told us proudly. He always enjoyed a tale of defiance. Now, with Grand-dad and the bulldog both long dead, characteristically Aunt Eliza still kept the bone. Grand-dad had died some years before I was born but Aunt Eliza had changed neither the office, the house, nor her own appearance during all those years. She managed the office single-handed, and when she wanted to go up the town to bank her takings she had to lock up. This, and putting on her hat, took time, and Aunt Eliza had never hurried in her life. 'Do you let them wait,' she said. Frequently the bank had closed by the time she got there. Not a bit put out, she tapped on the window with her umbrella and the manager had to come to the side door himself to let her in. I can only suppose that he found this the easiest course. It was quite impossible to argue with Aunt Eliza, or to thwart her. She believed that if she wanted to do something, then it must be acceptable, and she refused to take 'no' for an answer.

If Father had awakened in a good mood from his Sunday afternoon nap he would put his head round the door of the big room, where Mother was, and ask, 'Shall I go and get Eliza?' 'Yes, if you like,' Mother replied. She always said 'yes' although everyone's heart sank at the prospect of entertaining Aunt Eliza. Other than following Mother's tactful advice to shorten her skirts a little, Aunt Eliza followed the Edwardian fashions of her young days. She wore hats crowned with ostrich feathers which danced entrancingly as she sat in the front passenger seat of Father's car. Usually I went with him when he fetched her for Sunday tea, and I had a splendid view of her hats from my position on the back seat. She was very fussy, taking endless trouble with her clothes, and she would change a whole outfit at the last minute before going out rather than be seen with gloves of the wrong colour. Her corsets were unrelenting and her shoes so tight and high laced that she could not get them on without the help of what she called her 'shoe lift'. Aunt Eliza would not have felt dressed without a velvet band round her throat; she had different ones to match her dresses, and some had twinkly jewels sewn onto them. Naturally she came to tea in her best clothes, so she reeked of moth balls. I do not remember Aunt wearing spectacles, although her eyesight began to fail in late middle age. When she grew old her eyes got worse, and she became nearly blind. She confided to Mother that the doctor had told her she had 'catacombs' on her eyes.

When Father had driven Aunt Eliza from Lacton, ostrich plumes nodding all the way, and deposited her with Mother, he felt he had done his bit to entertain her, so he went off with the dog. This annoyed Mother. 'It's his sister,' she said. 'Why don't he stop and look after her?' The rare occasions when Father did try to amuse Aunt Eliza always turned out to be disasters. One summer Sunday we were playing with skipping ropes in the garden whilst Mother and Aunt Eliza sat watching from the summer house steps. Father came to join in our game: he took off his jacket and started to show off. Aunt Eliza disapproved. 'I say, we wouldn't do that at our age, would we Grace?' she asked Mother smugly. She was over twenty years older than Mother, who was beginning to feel plump and middle-aged at the time, and the remark made Mother wild. Just then Father tried to do some complicated trick with one of the skipping ropes, and got hit on the nose with a wooden handle. His nose swelled up, red from the bruise, and Aunt Eliza, ever tactless, felt bound to comment, 'Do you look at his old posteria, Grace!' she said. 'I say, do you look at his old posteria!' Mother started to laugh, and Father laughed too. He laughed so much that he had to stop playing with us. 'I've had enough,' he said. 'I'm all of a muck wash!' and he picked up his jacket and went back to the house to cool off.

If Father came in to tea when Aunt Eliza was with us he usually succeeded in making her cry. She wanted to please him, I suppose, at least she said she did. 'I study his temper,' she explained to Mother, 'I say, I study his temper.' However, she only managed to irritate him beyond measure. He would begin to tell some story; anxious to show her interest she felt obliged to join in and when he paused for breath she exclaimed, 'I know, I know.' If this was meant to encourage Father it had the opposite effect. 'If you know, I don't bloody well want to tell you, do I?' he'd say, and refuse to finish the tale. Aunt Eliza then started to dab her eyes with a small lacy handkerchief and Mother hurried to pass her some more tea. Aunt Eliza never quite grasped the fact that Father had three daughters. She had learnt the names of

Skinny and Milly before I was born and she used those two names for all three of us. She only came to our house on the occasional Sunday afternoons and at Christmas, but that was more than enough for us. She used to madden us girls. We always had the task of clearing the tea table and she insisted on trying to help us, or at least making a show of it. This she did by picking up a plate, a cup or the teapot, or whatever she could reach and presenting the objects to us one by one, saying, 'Come you along, Milly, you know where that go.'

Once a year, on Boxing Day, we went to tea at Aunt Eliza's house. First she came to lunch at Mill House, then we all drove in Father's car, through the early December dark, to Lacton. Aunt Eliza opened her back door with a huge key, and went in ahead of us to get the gas lights going. The house was terribly cold, having been left empty, without heating, all that day, and Christmas Day too, while Aunt visited us. The cold almost took my breath away. A tiny fire was lighted in the front room when we arrived but it soon went out. Aunt Eliza ignored it and Mother said she did not like to say anything, so we all sat there and shivered in our best velvet dresses, huddled round the fireplace looking at back copies of *The Tatler*. Meanwhile, our hostess put on a voluminous white apron and cut platefuls of bread and butter in the kitchen. I only have to see a copy of *The Tatler* now to feel that dire cold again and to be transported back to Aunt Eliza's front room at Lacton. In that room there were two hideous blue china ornaments on the mantelpiece. They had dangling blue painted glass bars suspended from them which moved and tinkled in the draught. They never stopped sounding. Our Boxing Day meal was laid in the dining room, which was little used and cold as charity. We had a splendid high tea with pressed ox tongue and pickles, trifle and cake, all prepared and left ready by Aunt Eliza's housekeeper before she went home for Christmas. We did not have high tea at home. Mother thought it was low class and, although Father complained bitterly, she insisted on afternoon tea when we came home from school, and supper later in the evening which, Father said, gave him indigestion. The high tea at Aunt Eliza's house was delicious and our enjoyment of it made up for the cold and boredom of the evening. Father carved the ox tongue, and Aunt Eliza served the trifle while Mother just sat and looked disapproving. She was a very unsatisfactory guest and made no attempt to enjoy the party fare. Father said that whenever she went out she just pingled with the food. He did justice to it himself. After tea Aunt Eliza opened a box of crackers and handed them out to us. We had to pull them, and then wear the paper hats which they had contained. Sometimes we found fireworks in the crackers, and Father helped us to light them in the kitchen, but more often we just got mottoes on little screws of paper, or riddles which I could not understand: 'Q. When is a door not a door? A. When it is a jar.'

When I was about five or six years old I asked Aunt Eliza if I could stay with her for a weekend. Mother was astounded; it seemed a crazy idea to her, but Aunt Eliza, to her credit, showed no dismay or surprise and agreed to have me as her guest. She was quite serious about it, which delighted me. Father took me in the car one Saturday, so that I could stay for Saturday night and most of Sunday, and I thoroughly enjoyed being the centre of attention. The spare bedroom where I slept was furnished with a majestic four-poster bed, too high for me to climb into it without Aunt's help. There was no bathroom; we had wash stands and chamber pots. Aunt Eliza drew my attention to the heavy white china pot, fluted and scrolled, standing conveniently under my bed. 'Do you use that,' she told me, 'if you just want to do number one.' During the night I rolled about in that big bed and eventually fell out on to the cold polished floor. Aunt Eliza came, carrying a candle to save lighting the gas, laughed, and put me back into bed again. She was dressed in a long white calico nightdress, and her hair hung down in two neat grey plaits. At that time, being a mollycoddled child, I had not learnt to tie bows, so that in the morning when I got dressed Aunt Eliza had to tie my shoe laces for me. She tied them so tightly that I could hardly walk, but walk I did, all the way up the town to the Congregational Chapel for Sunday morning worship. Aunt Eliza rarely missed attending chapel, and always went dressed in her best hat, ostrich plumes swaying as she walked along. We must have looked a strange pair. When Father had fetched me home Mother and my sisters asked me if I had enjoyed my rather unusual weekend, I was able to boast that I had seen Aunt Eliza in her nightgown with her hair down, which I felt sure was a unique experience. It had all been a very satisfactory adventure.

Although she did not dress fashionably, Aunt Eliza was immensely

interested in clothes. Mother complained that it was difficult to hold
a conversation with her because she was only interested in clothes and
Lacton society, and liked to discuss both endlessly. There were two
elderly matrons in Lacton who led the field, and were much admired
by Auntie. Anyone less grand she dismissed as 'no class, no class at all'.
Mother always dressed neatly; she wore a hat when she went out, and
gloves as well for church, and she tried to choose colours which suited
her, but there the matter ended. 'I don't want a lot of old jewellery,' she
said. Father would have liked her to wear diamonds and an Ascot hat,
and Aunt Eliza did her best to persuade Mother to that way of
thinking. 'I see old Mrs Cecil Morris at chapel this morning,' she said.
'My word, she'd got on a rare swanky hat. I say, that must have cost her
a pretty penny. I lay you a halfpenny she never got that under five
guineas. I reckon she bought that at Chamberlins of Norwich.' Mother
remained unmoved, even at the mention of such an expensive shop.
But there was worse to come. Sitting very upright, with her fingers
twiddling in her lap, Aunt Eliza began to tell Mother about Mrs Sadie
Walker's jumble sale. Mother disapproved of Sadie, who was the wife

of the Lacton cornchandler. There was always a flash of diamonds when Sadie shook hands, and she wore expensive 'figured silk' dresses. 'Getting herself up in all them old rings and that like,' Mother said, 'and having her hair all pleated up. I suppose she thinks she's someone.' Whatever Mother might say, Sadie was certainly a formidable lady and she ran all the charity events in Lacton. 'Just trying to get her name up,' Mother said. Aunt Eliza made a point of letting Mother know about Sadie's fund-raising successes so that Mother should realise that her own village efforts were puny by comparison. 'I say, old Sadie Walker is having a garden fête at hers next month,' she told Mother. 'I'll lay you a sovereign she'll make over three hundred pounds. I say, I reckon she'll make a rare lot more than what you could, Grace.' Father did not like to hear this any better than Mother did; he required success from his family. He did not want to be told that Mother could be 'bested' by anyone, least of all a rival corn-merchant's wife. The only subject Mother and Aunt Eliza ever agreed on was Father's badness. 'I say, I can't understand him, Grace,' said Aunt Eliza. 'That fare to me he isn't never happy time he isn't upsetting someone.' 'He's not right,' Mother declared. 'No, that he isn't,' Aunt Eliza agreed, 'I reckon he must have got a klink, do you mark my words; I say, I reckon he must have got a klink.'

Mother's father had been a flour miller, the manager of the mill where we lived until he died in early middle age. Then Father's father, Grand-dad, bought the mill to extend his business. Mother was already working in the mill office, and she remained there, to work for Grand-dad. I never knew Grand-dad, but I wish I had done so. It was he who started the family keeping pigs. During a farming depression before the first world war he found himself forced to accept a sty-ful of little pigs from a penniless farmer, in lieu of a bad debt. The pigs were in a terrible condition, near to starvation, as the farmer had run out of food stuffs. Grand-dad had them put in a shed and sent Father to feed them. When he opened the shed door Father was horrified to find that the pigs were eating one another, and he hurried back to tell the old man what was happening. 'Do you let the buggers be, boy,' Grand-dad said. 'They won't never get a cheaper meal!'

All his life Grand-dad supported the Liberal Party, and this was considered very daring in his younger days. He was a pugnacious devil, and at election time he sent poor Father to school wearing a large Liberal rosette. The other bigger boys beat him up, and when he got home covered in mud and with a bloody nose, Grand-dad decided on action. He was a very powerfully built man, medium in height, but broad-shouldered and ready for anything. He tied the rosette onto the bulldog's collar, and together they walked up and down the streets of Lacton, Grand-dad trailing his coat. Father said no one offered the old man a fight, and they dare not touch the bulldog to get the rosette off it, so that was how Grand-dad got the better of them. The bulldog went everywhere with Grand-dad. When he walked through the mill it ran ahead of him. Grand-dad taught it to do that, and sometimes sent the dog to run through the mill alone. The millers never knew if the dog was on its own or if Grand-dad was following it, so whenever they saw the bulldog coming they worked extra hard. This saved Grand-dad several trips through the mill and kept his workmen up to the mark. The strategy was typical of him.

Cows as well as horses were kept at the mill when Grand-dad was alive. On one occasion he went to buy a new cow, and he and the owner could not agree over the price. Grand-dad liked a bargain. 'I'll tell you what,' he said, 'I'll give you a sovereign for every inch between the cow's nose and the end of its tail.' The farmer was delighted; he thought he was about to make a good profit, but Grand-dad took the cow's head and its tail and bent the cow round so that there was only an inch left between the tip of the tail and the nose. 'Then the farmer had to beg Grand-dad to leave off,' Father told us, 'before the animal got its back broken.' Grand-dad must have been a remarkably strong man, and Father was rather proud of this story about him. Getting a cow for a sovereign was something to be proud of in itself.

The old man's second wife was strict chapel, and so of course was her daughter, Aunt Eliza, but Grand-dad did not fit in very well with chapel ideas, and one day he disgraced himself. He went into the Swan public house in Lacton for a drink at dinner time and raised his hand to salute a friend across the crowded room. He did not realise that the Swan was being auctioned that afternoon and his raised hand had constituted the final bid. He had to go home and tell Grandmother that he had bought a pub. Father used to tell us this with great glee, and I think he was delighted to remember his father's embarrassment.

Grandmother was a teetotaller, and she insisted that the wicked pub be sold again immediately. She would not hear of Grand-dad keeping it, even for a single day. Hearing Father talk, one would have supposed that there had not been much love lost between him and Grand-dad, although there must have been respect. I believe Father would have described the old man as a 'cross-grained old warmin' if he had not been dead. Showing respect for the dead was an important convention in those days and Father felt that his position demanded that he comply with it, so he assumed a special 'dead' voice when he spoke of Grand-dad. It seemed odd to me; it did not match up with his words.

Grand-dad never wore a collar and tie, always a red-and-white spotted handkerchief instead. He did not care what other people thought of him. He used to drive everywhere in a pony trap, and Father remembered how Grand-dad had taken it across Lacton Dam in the 1912 floods when no one else dare go through the water. 'The floods came up to the pony's middle,' Father said, 'but Grand-dad kept going.' The old man was a great drinker, so perhaps he got through the floods on Dutch courage. He was afflicted with gout and the doctor had to amputate one leg. 'You'll die if you keep drinking,' he told Grand-dad. 'I'll bloody well die if I stop!' was the reply, and the old man, equipped with a wooden leg, drank himself into his grave and enjoyed every minute of it. When he died he was buried in a shroud made out of mill boulting cloth and his coffin was carried to the funeral in one of his own horse-drawn wagons. It must have been quite a spectacle for the neighbourhood.

Keeping on good terms with the neighbours was beneath Grand-dad. There was one old woman, living not far from the mill, who was his arch enemy. She had got the better of him in some transaction and he never forgave her. During her lifetime she drove everywhere in a cart pulled by one horse and one mule. When she died Grand-dad, who did not have Father's respect for the dead, made up a rhyme about her.

'Old Mrs Beckett, in her wooden jacket,
She neither drove horses nor mules.
She lived like a hog and she died like a dog,
And she left all her money to fools!'

Grand-dad used to sing this as loudly as possible when he drove his pony trap past the farm where she had once lived. Presumably he did it for the befit of her heirs, and his own satisfaction.

When Grand-dad and Father first saw Mother they both took a great fancy to her. She must have looked lovely, for she had the most beautiful colouring, wavy chestnut hair, dark brown eyes, and a pink and white complexion. Her long hair was piled on top of her head in a big bun, and she wore frilly, lacy white blouses and long skirts with tight belts which the Edwardian ladies favoured. Father used to chase Mother round the mill buildings. She held up her long skirts and ran, but not too fast because the game was for Father to catch her. In later years, when he felt a twinge of romance, Father would remind her of this time when he was courting her. 'Do you mind the times I used to run you round the buildings?' he asked fondly. Sometimes Mother just smiled and said, yes, she remembered, but now and then she replied with some spirit, 'I never needed to let you get me. I could always run better than you.'

Under Mother's delightful exterior she hid a calculating mind and a head which always ruled her heart. Whether Grand-dad realised this or not, he was so enamoured that he proposed marriage to her. She refused him and married Father instead. After the marriage Grand-dad still felt a soft spot for Mother even though she failed to produce the grandsons he required of her. When her first daughter was born he said, 'That'll have to be named De-*bore*-ah.' Mother was not having any of that, she told us, and she chose a different name for Skinny. Grand-dad, who liked to see a show of spirit, did not hold it against her, and consented to be photographed with his baby grand-daughter sitting on his one good knee. He followed this up by giving Mother a dog, a 'spanel' which he said had to be named Kruger. Mother gave in gracefully this time and Kruger it became. Father said she preferred 'that bloody dog' to him, she made such a fuss of it. One day he felt so jealous that he lost his temper and grabbed Kruger and gave him a thrashing, holding him up by his tail. Mother came upon the scene. 'If you don't let go of my dog I'll throw this stone at you!' she threatened. Father had no opinion of her aim and he kept on hitting the dog, so Mother threw the stone and caught Father on the side of the head. Blood poured down his face and he yelled and clapped his hand to his wounded head, but he let go of Kruger. 'That served him right,' Mother told us when she recounted the story. 'He never thought I'd get him. He shouldn't have touched my dog.' Father carried the scar of that encounter to his dying day.

Whenever Father and Mother quarrelled about money, which they did frequently, Mother said, 'I ought to have married your father, then I'd have had all the money. I was a fool to marry you instead of him; I could have had him if I'd liked. I should have been an old man's darling, that's what I should have been.' 'Better to be an old man's darling than a young man's slave,' she quoted. Usually Father could give as good as he got in their quarrels, but he could never find an answer to this taunt. It just sent him into one of his rages, and he did not come in to meals for several days. I imagine he thought he was punishing the household, but really it was an enormous relief to us children; meals with both parents present always ended in rows.

IV

Mother was quite a good cook, and she taught a succession of maids to do some of the cooking, so meals should have been easy for her, but they were not. Anything to do with food always sparked off a row, or at least some argument, between my parents.

When Father was not keeping an eye on the mill or the office, or going to the local markets, he went off in his car on his 'rounds'. This meant visiting all the shops and businesses which dealt with him and chatting up the owners. He took orders for anything from flour to dog biscuits and seed corn. On alternate Mondays, regular as clockwork, it was the 'long round', and Mother had to cut sandwiches for Father and Uncle Teddie, who went off together on a round which lasted all day. She never trusted Uncle Teddie's wife to provide the packed lunch, and she usually made salt beef sandwiches, with plenty of mustard, to please Father. There was a bit of a scramble getting the two men away on time, but it was worth it because after they had gone Mother could enjoy one of the few days when she was not tied to cooking a man-sized mid-day dinner. As the door closed on Father she could be seen visibly to relax and begin to think about giving us potatoes boiled in their skins for dinner, which we adored and Father loathed.

Father got furious if one of us was even slightly late for a meal. As someone usually managed to be late, he was put in a bad mood from the beginning, but in any case being cooped up in a room together for half an hour at a stretch was more than my parents could stand, and always, at every dinner time, they had a row. Sometimes Mother would make a great effort over dinner, providing one of Father's favourite dishes, a steaming apple pudding into which he poured an eggcupful of gin, like a ritual offering, before the pudding was cut and served. He would start eating this delicacy and enjoy it so much that his mind would go to past gastronomic joys, and re-membering happily he would remark, 'Tell you what, that's a rare long time since we had pig's pluck.' At once Mother was incensed. 'Here I go to all this trouble making you apple pudding,' she said, ' and all you can say is you want pig's pluck; you're never satisfied!' Then off they would go, hammer and tongs. The result was that Father missed his meals for the next few days, this being his habitual method of punishing both Mother and himself; but he never starved. For a start he never missed breakfast, but wolfed it down in angry silence. After that he relied on raiding the larder, which he did regularly, for supplies of bread and cheese, pickled onions, sausage rolls, or any other cold food which came to hand. Mother could never go to the pantry and be sure to find a cold pie she had put away for the next day's supper. Quite often it had vanished overnight, which made catering difficult for her, to say the least. If she complained Father said, 'That's a masterpiece to me, go to hell if that isn't, if a man can't have a mite of bread and cheese in his own house when he have a mind for it.'

Not only was Father unpredictable in his eating habits, but he also used to bring home highly perishable foods at inconvenient times, or forget to bring them when Mother was expecting them. Fish caused the most trouble. There was no fish shop in Lacton. Mother said it was impossible to buy nice fish in the town. Once a week our regular ice man became the fish man and had a stall in the market. He was usually well laced with whisky and he breathed the fumes all over his fish and his customers. Because he was so often a bit the worse for drink, his knife was inclined to slip when he filleted the plaice, and he often cut himself. He bound up his cut fingers in questionable-looking rags, and as he had to keep handling the wet fish he needed to find some means of protecting the bandages, which he did by wearing condoms over them. It may have been seeing these waving about as he parcelled up the fish which put Mother off; anyway she never bought fish herself. Instead, when Father went to Norwich or Beccles market, she relied on him bringing some home. If he would bring any, of what sort and in what quantity if he did, was always open to speculation. Only one thing was certain: he never did the right thing for Mother. There was either no fish, and Mother had not much else to fall back on, or there was a houseful of food and an excess of fish as well. Although Mother knew better than to expect any co-operation on Father's part, she still complained bitterly about it.

Father was very fond of meat and he was always ready to criticise a roasted joint. His old school friend, Harry Taylor, was our butcher and Father held him personally responsible for sending the correct meat. Mother did not go into the butcher's shop, select a piece of meat and carry it home with her. In those days everything was ordered and delivered. She used to ask for a lean joint because she did not like fat herself and neither did we children. Next day Father saw Harry Taylor in Lacton and complained that there was not enough fat on his meat, so the joints which Harry sent to the Mill House alternated between very fat and very lean, and whichever he sent was wrong. When my parents confronted each other across the joint of meat there was always trouble. 'There isn't a mite of fat on here,' Father said, brandishing a knife over the dish. 'Wait till I go into Lacton, I'll swear holes through Harry Taylor!' For some reason this threat made a deep impression on me and when I went into the butcher's shop with Mother I expected to see Harry Taylor full of holes. I imagined his white coat overall positively perforated and was mystified when he looked just the same as usual.

Another argument indulged in by my parents at the dinner table was about who should carve. Father thought it was his right and liked to take the opportunity to put on each person's plate the pieces which he knew they most disliked. When we objected to this treatment he told us to eat what we were given and be thankful. 'Them what don't want to eat it can rub it over themselves,' he added. Father's methods created such a fuss that Mother tried to keep the peace by starting to carve before Father could do so. On one occasion he took up the knife before she did, and when she demanded that he should give it to her, he, in a fit of fury, placed the blade in his hand with the cutting edge to his palm and, holding out his clenched fist with the knife handle towards Mother, said, 'All right, if you want it, take it!' Mother did not hesitate. She seized the handle of the knife and pulled. It laid open Father's palm, and iodine and bandages were called for. They managed without having the wound stitched, but I think they frightened even themselves that time.

Until I went to school I had never eaten a rice pudding which was not made with eggs. Father kept an odd assortment of chickens and ducks running about the orchard beside the mill roadway. They were all kinds and colours, but they must have laid well because one of the mill men used to bring in quantities of eggs every day to be washed by the maid and stored in the pantry. Mother had a big white enamel pail of preserved eggs which she put down every summer, when eggs were most plentiful. There were ducks' eggs, as well as hens', and Father liked to have the duck eggs for his breakfast. Mother refused to touch them; she said they were strong old things. On the lawn behind the house we had hen coops each summer, where baby chickens and ducklings were cherished by fat brown hens. Often there was a wire netting run filled with little goslings which I loved best of all. Father kept a lot of geese, but they were on a water meadow at the back of the mill, not in the orchard with the other poultry. If Father and I went across that meadow together he said, 'Mind where you walk, girl, them buggers shit by guesswork.' I never went near the geese on my own because I was terrified of the gander. It once pecked a piece out of Father's leg when he went to take eggs from the geese, and he swore so long and loudly about it that he made sure no one could forget it. The day Father got pecked, as soon as he reached the house and a comfortable chair to sit on, he rolled up his trouser leg to show us the damage. There was a patch of blood. 'Do you look where that bugger got me!' he said. At intervals after that he showed us the scar. 'That's where that bloody old gander got me,' he told us, in case we needed to be reminded.

As well as chickens, ducks and goslings in the garden, we children kept tortoises. At the beginning we had one each, bought in Norwich market, but Milly's did not live more than a year. Skinny's and mine lived to a ripe old age, but Skinny soon lost interest in tortoises, so Milly took over, and she and I became very fond of them. They were called Isaiah and Angeline. They were continually escaping, and once Isaiah was found walking down the middle of the road by the church. Everyone living nearby knew to whom he belonged, and he was brought home in disgrace. The other tortoise, Angeline, was not such a long-distance walker. When she escaped she did not go far, but set about eating Mother's flowers, and destroyed several favourite plants, so that Mother got angry with us about it. I suppose it was the sight of the goslings in their wire-netting pen which made us think of asking for a tortoise run. Father said it was 'a lot of old squit', and nothing got done about it, but we kept on asking. One day the flower-eating tortoise had been more destructive than usual and we countered Mother's indignation by begging once more for a means to keep the tortoises from straying. Mother was fed up. 'I'll make you a tortoise run,' she

said. 'My grandfather was a wheelwright and I know how to make that sort of thing.' She marched off to the carpenter's shop behind the mill office, with Milly and me trailing along, following her. She soon found some suitable planks lying around and she cut two short sides and two long ones out of them. She seemed expert, and we watched as she nailed the pieces together. Mother must have been a woman in a hundred too, for she certainly knew how to drive a nail. When she had finished she stood back in triumph. Suddenly we all realised that she had constructed the tortoise run round the carpenter's bench, and we could not get it off. At that moment Bob came into the carpenter's shop; no doubt he knew we were there and had heard our pleased voices turn to dismayed ones. Bob must have seen at a glance what Mother had done, but he did not laugh, only his blue eyes twinkled a little more than usual. 'Never you mind, ma'am,' he said kindly, 'that don't signify. Do you hold hard a minute time I get that off and we'll soon have that right.' Then he took the run apart and freed it from the bench while we watched him. He proceeded to fix it together again, nailing cunning little splines across the four corners to keep it rigid. He promised not to tell Father that he had helped us and we carried the run across the yard in great delight. In no time it was on the lawn with the two tortoises inside it. When Father came into the garden that evening he saw it. 'Who made that there?' he asked. 'I did,' Mother replied, preening herself. 'You never thought of them cross-pieces,' Father observed smugly; so Mother owned up to her escapade and told him how Bob had come to her rescue after she got the tortoise run stuck fast round the carpenter's bench. Father was delighted: he laughed and laughed, and strangely Mother did not take offence.

One of the most interesting and lucrative things Father had at the mill was his eel trap. I used to be taken by lantern light to see the baby elvers as they passed through the river under the mill. The water was black with the tiny wriggling things. Later, when they had grown into big fine eels, they returned, and we saw them collected from the trap and emptied into wire-netting-sided crates which were hung into the river on chains. Father hauled them up to show us what a lot of eels he had got. We could not see the eels go into the trap because they were caught as they went through the mill race, where the water churned white. When his crates were full, Father raised them all from the water and set the men to packing the eels for the train journey to London. He had special wooden trays with holes in them and they packed these, a layer of eels and a layer of ice, in travelling boxes, which kept the eels fresh and alive until they were eaten. All the mill cats used to congregate and watch the eels being packed, and we watched too. Occasionally there was an eel which was not considered big enough to send to London with the others, and Father threw it to the cats. They ate it after a lot of fuss and excitement killing it. He usually brought a few eels into the house for Mother to cook, which she did, under protest. She told us that some of the most expensive restaurants in London served Father's eels, but that did not make her like the job of cooking them herself. Father could hold an eel in the first two fingers of his left hand, while he skinned it, which was no mean achievement. I never saw anyone else who could do it. Later he damaged a finger by catching it in a piece of mill machinery, and after that he had to pin down the eels before he could skin them, just as ordinary people did.

Eels were not the only thing Mother hated to cook; indeed although she was a capable cook she did not enjoy the work. Eels jumped out of the saucepan, she said, and they were horrible old things. I never tasted one as a child, as she took it for granted that we should follow her taste in food, not Father's. She told us the things she disliked were nasty until we believed it. Father sometimes brought home tripe from a stall in Norwich market, and again Mother disapproved, and with the same result: I never tasted it. It certainly looked very odd, and Father ate it with vinegar which I knew I disliked because I had tried that. Occasionally, on our walks over the fen, Father and I collected what he called 'mushrunes'. We put them in his hat and carried them home, where he taught me how to peel them and twist out the stalks. If Mother fried the mushrooms we all ate them, but Father declared that they were spoilt, although he did not say this until after he had consumed his share. He wanted them cooked in a kind of milky stew which he ate out of a big white basin. He absolutely loved this, and made a lot of noise spooning it up, which caused Mother to protest that he 'slooped' his food, and to start another row between them.

Father disliked cows. He said he had had a bellyful of looking after cows when Granddad was alive, so he did not keep one for the house. Instead milk was delivered every morning. It came in a metal milk churn, carried by pony cart to our door by Ned, a neighbouring farmer. Ned had long-handled brass measures for a pint and a half-pint and with these he ladled out the milk into a jug held by one of the maids. Father took a great dislike to Ned, chiefly, I suspect, because he was ineffectual, poor, and did not farm his land well. He called Ned 'that bloody blue-faced monkey' on account of the blue-black beard stubble which covered his chin, no matter whether he shaved or not. Maybe Father's feelings about Ned were influenced by the fact that the milk was of very uncertain quality, or maybe he just did not like the look of the man. Once the milk came to the breakfast table tasting strongly of disinfectant, and Mother tackled Ned about it. 'Yes,' he said, 'we did have the disinfectant about because the old cow calved yesterday.' He did not think apologies were necessary, and he did not offer any. That was enough to upset Mother, but there was worse to come. A few weeks later the milk arrived grey and gritty. This was too much and Father undertook to give Ned a piece of his mind, but the farmer remained unmoved. 'I reckon the old cow must have put her foot in the bucket,' he said. After that Father said Ned was getting too independent and Mother had to change to another milkman. 'We've had enough of his old buck,' she said.

Mother was a most orderly housekeeper. The household bills came in once a month, and there were dressmakers' bills and Norwich outfitters' accounts too. Mother prided herself on her office training and all receipts were strung on bill hooks and hung up under the pantry shelves. When things became too much for Father and he felt he was beset by bills and women in that household with such a strong female bias, he would drop his hands to hang limply at his sides in despair and say, 'I'm fed up! I'm fed up with the whole issue!' If things were extra bad he would say, 'I'm fed up with the whole bloody issue, go to hell if I aren't!' and stump off. Then it was time to keep out of his way until he felt better. If he complained about the household bills, Mother used to harden her lips into a prim line and say, 'Very well, we'll economise. There'll be no more lavatory paper bought in this house. You'll have to use sugar paper.' (She meant the thick blue paper which grocers used for sugar bags. In the village shop sugar was weighed on brass scales and bagged up in blue paper as it was sold.) For some reason this threat always subdued Father, and he gave in at once. 'Oh blast, no!' he would say. 'Not sugar paper! For God's sake don't you do that!'

V

Because Father's sister Aunt Eliza lived near us, and he felt responsible for her, she was the relative we saw most often and knew best; nevertheless we had a lot of Mother's family to contend with as well. Most of them lived too far away to come to see us very frequently, so when they did come they stayed in the house. Mother made a great event of each visit. She wanted to have everything nice, she said, and of course she wanted to show how well she had done for herself, marrying money. The house was given extra cleaning; there were clean windows, clean table cloths, and clean children, and she cooked, and cooked, and cooked. Uncle Laurence and Aunt Georgina came to stay for a fortnight every summer. Aunt Georgina was Mother's real aunt, but Uncle Laurence was only an uncle because he had married her, and Mother made this quite clear. The old lady looked very like Mother. She had the same features and the same brown eyes, but grey hair done up in a bun on top of her head in Edwardian style. She was not quite so old-fashioned in her appearance as Aunt Eliza, and her dark skirts were only moderately long. She always wore velvet neck bands, and usually small earrings and strings of pearls as well. Aunt Georgina loved jewellery and could not understand Mother's indifference to it. When she came she often brought a ring or a locket for Mother. 'This belonged to your Great Aunt Anne, dear,' she would say, and Mother would thank her and put the piece in her jewel case and never take it out again. Uncle Laurence was a Methodist, so Aunt Georgina was one by marriage, and they became pillars of their local chapel. Uncle Laurence almost ran the whole thing and, as he contributed generously to every fund, including the minister's pay packet, he felt entitled to tell the poor man not only what texts to take for his sermons, but also what subjects should not be mentioned in them. Luckily, being Methodists, they had a fresh minister every few years so no doubt the thought of the coming move helped the unfortunate incumbents to stay sane whilst they worked in Uncle's district.

Uncle Laurence had been a pork butcher, and it was not until he retired from work that he married Aunt Georgina and took up bossing the chapel as his hobby. In his business capacity he had visited farms to buy up pigs and had taken a lively interest in the current misfortunes of farming. He liked nothing better than to tell us at length all the mistakes the farmers had made, and he savoured his memories of butchery as it used to be when he was a young man in his shop, putting the farmers right if their pigs were not up to standard. When he got too excited and went so far as to mention a sow farrowing, Aunt Georgina rebuked him. 'Now, dear,' she said, 'there's no need to go too far into the details of farm life.' At that he stopped obediently, but on the whole he remained irrepressible. He insisted on referring to his wife as 'my old Dutch'. Aunt Georgina put up a good show of indignation when he did so, but really she liked him to be what she thought of as a little coarse and frank; it made her feel all the more feminine. On one occasion when Milly was blundering about he remarked happily, 'She waller about like a bladder of lard!' Milly was a large gawky girl when she was in her early teens, and liable to fall over her own feet, so she could not forgive him for this well-placed insult.

Uncle was a very fine-looking old man, as I remember him, with brilliant blue eyes and stiff brush of white hair standing straight up on top of his head. He wore black lace-up boots and a black suit with an elegant gold watch chain across his waistcoat. His shirts were white, with starched collars. I never saw him take his jacket off and although, like Father, he had a straw hat for summer, his was a rakish boater. Strangely enough, although they had little in common, Father seemed willing to tolerate Uncle Laurence. The old man saw right through Father's dramatic exhibitions and ruses to get his own way, and was not intimidated by them. In fact, if Father was in a bad mood, one dry caustic comment from Uncle Laurence could set him smiling again, so Uncle was a useful person to have around the place.

Mother had a lot of sisters and brothers. The one we saw regularly was her youngest brother, Uncle Teddie, who worked with Father and lived in the village. Uncle Teddie had been a soldier in the Great War, and he was a very exciting person because he had a motor bike. Sometimes he took Milly on the back of it and they went to swim at Great Yarmouth pool. I always found him rather unnerving, as he had a nasty way of asking awkward questions. 'How many fingers have you got on one hand?' he asked me. 'Five,' I replied proudly. 'No, you haven't,' he said, 'you've got four fingers and one thumb,' and he laughed because he had caught me out. I used to get behind Mother when he was with us, and hope to remain unnoticed. Uncle Teddie kept pigeons, and he gave me a beautiful brown-and-white one called Daisy. She had a habit of alighting on my head. I did not like the feel of her feet in my hair, but I had not got the courage to admit it; however Father probably realised that I was not too fond of Daisy, and she was allowed to fade out of my life. She must have been discreetly returned to Uncle Teddie.

Aunt Connie was Uncle Teddie's wife. She was a tiny person, with beautiful curling black hair and huge eyes, given to wearing 'pneumonia-necked' blouses which Aunt Georgina thought were not quite nice. Aunt Georgina said that Uncle Teddie's Aunt Connie had made a dead set at him to get him to marry her. He kept a big Airedale terrier, and he used to take it out with him, running behind his motor bike. His future wife was a school teacher, and one day when she was on playground duty at the school she came to the railings as Uncle Teddie and the dog dashed past, and called to him to stop. She told him he was cruel to make the dog run so fast. That was the beginning of the romance, and clearly Uncle Teddie adored her. After they got married he bought a side-car so that she could ride with him, and they left the dog at home. As Mother had a sister called Connie, in order to avoid confusion Uncle Teddie's wife was known as Uncle Teddie's Aunt Connie, and no one made any attempt to shorten it. She ruled Uncle Teddie with a rod of iron, so much so that the grown-ups all said they felt sorry for him. When she visited us she was all done up in a navy suit, and she wore gloves, even in summer, and when she was not going to church, and of course she wore one of her offending blouses, usually made of oyster-coloured satin. She had unlikely shoes for the country; they had what we girls called 'lavatory heels', and her hair was put into a big bun at the back of her head, with wispy, provocative side curls. I could never decide if it was coming down or if it was meant to be like that.

When we saw her in her own home, Uncle Teddie's Aunt Connie was dressed in an old flowered pinarette, much the worse for wear, with her skinny white arms protruding from the ample armholes. On her feet she had scruffy black plimsolls, and her hair really was coming down. Uncle Teddie kept several hundred white chickens, and she spent her days cooking something for them or the children, or heating pans of water on the ancient kitchen range. When Aunt Georgina was a guest in the house she was terribly shocked because Uncle Teddie's Aunt Connie bathed the baby in a tin bath on the kitchen table, and then, in full view of everyone, shamelessly proceeded to wash the baby's clothes in the dirty bathwater. Mother said perhaps Connie did it to get rid of Aunt Georgina. It must have made a contrast to staying in Mother's house. Aunt Georgina did not understand that country people could not afford to waste water, coming as she did from the heart of Ipswich, or she might have had more sympathy for Uncle Teddie's Aunt Connie. Everyone said that Uncle Teddie worked too hard, keeping all those chickens as well as doing his job with Father. He was never known to stop working, and his wife must have had a dreary existence. One day she came to Mother and said, 'Gracie, I believe Teddie's leading a double life!' What prompted this was not disclosed. Mother dealt with it in her customary manner of supreme authority. 'Don't be silly, Connie,' she said, 'the boy doesn't have time.' The matter ended there and Uncle Teddie's Aunt Connie accepted this very unflattering reassurance.

Mother's sister, who was also called Connie, lived in London and was married to an enormous cockney, whom we all knew simply as Batesy. He had a passion for sausage rolls and before he came to the Mill House Mother used to bake dozens and dozens of them, and he always ate the lot. She used to get furious about it because she would have liked her baking to last, and not get eaten up quickly. Poor Mother! In this she could not win. Give or take a few sausage rolls, Batesy weighed twenty stone. Harassed shop-keepers used to beg him not to get on to the weighing machines which they kept outside their shops, because they were afraid he might break them, and Batesy delighted in the anxiety he caused. He liked to march purposefully up to any and every weighing machine he could find, just for the fun of giving the owners a fright. Batesy's job in London was building caravans. He had once made one for the royal household and had a photograph of it being towed through the gates of Buckingham Palace. He carried the picture with him everywhere he went, carefully tucked into the back of his wallet, and he did not require much encouragement to take it out and hand it round to be admired.

56

Aunt Connie was red-faced and ginger-haired, not a bit like Mother. She wore gold pince-nez and used to sit at the piano and play and sing all the current musical hits, with many trills and much feeling. It made quite a change from 'Abide with me', Mother's favourite hymn. The drawing room was a different place with Aunt Connie at the piano. Jack, who was one of Father's office clerks, was quite an authority on the Charleston, and taught it to us in the kitchen on Saturday evenings in the wintertime. He could cross and uncross his hands over his bent knees in the best style, and I was thrilled when I learned to copy him, but even he did not sing like Aunt Connie. As well as singing, Aunt Connie had a splendid talent for sewing, and she made dresses for my dolls in all the latest fashions, some with uneven hemlines like those in the dressmaking magazines. I adored her. When she invited Mother and me to stay with her in London I counted the days until we went. In London Aunt Connie had a big cardboard 'W' which she placed in the front room window so that when the Walls ice cream man came pedalling along with his barrow he saw it, and stopped and rang his bell. Aunt Connie would then go out to buy ice cream from him for lunch. I was told in advance about this highly sophisticated procedure and was all keyed up for it because I thought the man would carry a wall of ice cream round with him and hack off a piece to sell, and I was longing to see him do it. It was a terrible let-down to find that he only sold wafers and cornets. Ice cream brought to the door was not the only modern convenience Aunt Connie had in London. She quite made up for the lack of walls of ice cream when she produced an ancient pair of curling tongs which she heated over the gas and used for curling Mother's hair and her own before going to the theatre. It was a spell-binding slight. There was a smell of singeing hair, and I was allowed to stand on the bed, the better to be able to see what she was doing. She never said, 'Mind the way!' to me at all.

As well as Aunt Connie in London, Mother had a very much younger sister, Aunt Rose, who was making a career in nursing and worked in one of the big London teaching hospitals. Aunt Rose was very lively and modern. She was courted by at least half a dozen eligible men, and went out to dances and London theatres, dressed in very fashionable and expensive evening gowns. Aunt Georgina got quite worried about it. 'I can't understand it, dear,' she said to Mother. 'Rose never gets married but she always seems to be on the verge.' After a time Aunt Rose rejected all her younger suitors and settled for a rich 'Sugar Daddy' twice her age. He bought her diamonds and pearls, real ones, and took her to the continent for holidays, but she never married him. It was a shocking but enviable state of affairs. He was a photographer, and sometimes Aunt Rose let us see the pictures he had taken of her. There was one of which Aunt Georgina deeply disapproved. It was a beautiful portrait, showing Rose's head in profile, and one plump bare shoulder. The rest of her disappeared into a white mist. Aunt Georgina said, 'I don't think it's quite modest, dear. That looks as if she might have got nothing on. It would have been nicer if he had put in just a little piece of lace.'

Aunt Rose brought her Sugar Daddy to visit us at the Mill House. They both came to stay. He proved to be a small, wizened little monkey of a man, not very prepossessing, but Aunt Rose said he was a gentleman. I had been told that he wore a top hat in London when he took Aunt Rose out, but he did not bring it with him to the country. This was a big disappointment to me, but he made up for it by wearing spats, and to my amazement he refused to go to church. He had the nerve to say, 'No, thank you,' when Mother suggested it on Sunday morning.

The most fascinating relation Mother had was Uncle John. He was a black sheep. Years ago he had gone to West Africa to work, and married a French lady, Auntie Mimi. He only came home to England twice during my childhood but each visit was an excitement in itself and quite unforgettable. The first time he came he brought Auntie Mimi with him. They used to swear at one another in French, or so we thought. She wore black town suits and very high-heeled shoes which made her stumble on our stony paths, and she could scarcely speak a word of English. Most astounding of all, she wore a lot of make-up, and her long face was powdered dead white. She had one of those fox furs which have legs and tail dangling, and the face bites on to the end of the back to keep the fur clasped round the wearer's shoulders. The eyes were very glassy but it was none the less impressive for that. None of us children had seen anything like it before. When she came to stay at the Mill House Auntie Mimi brought her Pekinese dog with her. It was a loathsome coddled creature, called Bogy, and much against her will Mother was forced to allow it in the bedroom. Bogy took a terrible dislike to his new surroundings, and as a protest got under the big double bed and crouched there against the farthest wall. He was deaf to all Auntie Mimi's tears and entreaties - in French - and no one could get him to come out. Finally Uncle Teddie volunteered to try, and managed to crawl under the bed and pull Bogy out by the tail. Luckily he did not get bitten, but Auntie Mimi was furious, not grateful at all. She thought Uncle Teddie had deserved to be bitten for pulling her darling dog's tail.

No one could have called Uncle John's and Auntie Mimi's visit a happy one. Because she was a Frenchwoman, Mother explained to us, Auntie Mimi always drank wine at meals, so it was nothing short of a disaster when Skinny filled Auntie Mimi's glass with drinking water at the start of our guest's first meal with us. Mother did not know what to do. She did not have any wine in the house, at least not any table wine. 'A glass of wine' meant port or sherry on a Sunday morning after church, so Auntie Mimi was left to look in horror at the water in her glass, while Mother glared at Skinny, and no one said a word, until afterwards.

The next time Uncle John came he arrived alone. Mother told us that Auntie Mimi had left him, and while he was in the house we were on no account to be heard singing the popular song,

'She was a dear little dicky bird,
Cheep, cheep she went.
Sweetly she sang to me, till all my money was spent.
I went o'er the shore, and we parted on fighting terms.
She was one of the early birds,
And I was one of the worms.

After that, of course, Milly and I kept chanting it to ourselves in our bedroom and giggling. Apparently not only had Uncle John's wife left him, but she had spent all his money before doing so. It was a very shocking thing, and the grown-ups shut themselves away for hours, and discussed it both with and without Uncle John. Aunt Georgina came to stay and added her voice to the general disapproval. She felt that she was head of the family, and after one of their lengthy discussions she said, 'Well, John dear, I shall be glad to give you some more advice if you feel you need it,' and he replied, 'Advice is cheap!' and banged out of the room. Mother was deeply shocked. 'Fancy speaking like that to his own aunt!' she said. Uncle John had put an announcement in the newspaper to say that he would not (indeed could not) be responsible for any more of his wife's debts. Aunt Georgina considered this to be a terrible disgrace for the family. 'Well, did you ever, dear?' she said.

In Father's opinion Uncle John was an effeminate sponger. He had not made much money, or made a success of his life at all, and, Father said, he had let himself be buggered about by a woman. Father maintained that a man should always keep the eleventh commandment, which was not to let himself be buggered about. As he seemed to have nowhere to go, Uncle John stayed with us at the Mill House for weeks and weeks. Every day when Father came in to dinner, there the bounder was, not even properly dressed, but sitting in the best chair, wearing a red silk dressing gown and drinking Father's whisky. Uncle John was the first man I ever knew to own a dressing gown, let alone wear one at mid-day and not get dressed before breakfast. As if this were not enough to damn him, Uncle John had a big bottle of mimosa perfume, which he used lavishly. 'Stinking himself up,' Father called it.

Uncle John's luggage consisted of five trunkfuls of clothes and books, and Mother had no space for it; it cluttered up the house. Those trunks contained some very desirable things. There was a solar topee which I was allowed to wear while I pranced round his bedroom. When Uncle John did get dressed it was in a pure silk shirt and expensive linen suit, with brown-and-white brogues and a panama hat. He liked to carry a walking stick and sometimes he invited me to accompany him on his rather careful walks. He only went if the weather was fine and there was no mud. He found a moorhen's nest and showed it to me. I liked him, but clearly Father did not, and Mother was worried to death because Uncle John just stayed and stayed. He could not go, she explained to us, because he had no money to pay his fare back to Africa. He kept asking Mother to lend him money, but Father said Uncle John was a nice beauty trying to sponge off a woman, and he forbade Mother to part with any of her savings. There were terrible scenes. In the end the relations clubbed together to pay Uncle John's fare and get him out of the country. Mother said they had all

had just about enough of his old buck, and they had to get rid of him somehow before he ate them out of house and home.

So Uncle John set off with all his trunks and boxes, escorted to the village station by Uncle Teddie, who had received strict instructions from Mother to see that the Black Sheep got on to the train and, whatever happened, to come back without him. When they got to the station Uncle John borrowed a shilling from Uncle Teddie and gave it to the porter, thus proving himself a cad and a bounder to the bitter end. Mother said sixpence would have done nicely. 'He got a shilling out of that poor boy just so as he could swank,' she said. 'He knew Teddie hadn't got much money.' She could not get over it, but Father did not seem surprised. 'That weren't as if you didn't know what he was,' he told her. When it was discovered that Uncle John had left his solar topee behind, Mother refused to send it on to him. Instead, as a final indignity, she let it go into the dressing-up chest for when we played charades. 'Serve him right!' she said.

VI

The only one of my parents' friends who ever stayed at the Mill House was Uncle Bernie. He was not a real uncle, but it was the fashion then for children to call their parent's friends Uncle or Aunt. Christian names would have sounded too familiar and surnames were thought too distant, so we acquired a lot of false uncles and aunts. Uncle Bernie was a passionate lover of Norfolk, its wild life, history and dialect. Sometimes he could be very interesting with the tales he told about his childhood but more often than not I got fed up with Norfolk before he had finished with it and looked upon him as a bit of a crank, and a rather boring one at that. He and his brothers had known Father and Mother since their young days, when Bernie's uncle used to bring the boys to the mill on fishing expeditions. (There was excellent fishing to be had in the millpond, and people would knock on our kitchen door and ask permission to fish, which was always given, provided, Father said, they behaved themselves.) Uncle Bernie was only a few years older than my father, and as I first remember him he was supposed to be a carefree bachelor, if an ageing one. He had false teeth and sometimes retired to bed with migraine. During my early childhood illness amongst us was rare, and it was odd to see a grown-up person with a headache lying in a darkened room.

At one time Mother had taken a Red Cross course in first aid and home nursing so she rather enjoyed Uncle Bernie's migraines. It gave her a chance to try her hand on a patient who was not one of the family. Mother and some of the neighbours attended first aid classes together, and on winter evenings they all met at our house to practise bandaging. Skinny and I had to act as casualties, and we were bandaged and re-bandaged before the day of Mother's examination came round. She passed with flying colours, and after that she seemed to like bandaging us whenever we needed it. She dealt with all our smaller cuts and bruises; anything serious called for Father's attention. Milly was the most accident-prone , and Father had to mop up her blood and take her to the doctor to be stitched or encased in plaster. Father put iodine on our cuts and arnica on our sprains and that covered all necessary first aid in the house. The arnica was in a small brown bottle and Father painted it on to the skin with a little brush. It felt beautifully cool and comforting.

We went through measles, and all the usual children's ailments. Mother used to come to see me as I languished in bed. 'I don't like the look of you,' she said. When Father came in to dinner he too would come and stand at the foot of my bed. 'She don't look none too fierce to me,' he told Mother. 'You'd better go across and send for the doctor.' There was no telephone in the house and Mother had to go across the yard to use the instrument in the mill office. Mother's favourite doctor was Dr Rodwell, who had delivered all her babies; she had confidence in him, but I preferred his younger partner, Simmy.

The doctor came when he was summoned, in those times, by people who could pay his bills. Those who could not pay did not send for him except in desperate circumstances. Before the doctor came Mother put clean sheets on the bed and a clean nightdress on the patient. When he arrived she used her special voice and went very prim. Father had to collect our medicine which was made up in the doctor's surgery in Lacton. If Simmy had been to see me he sometimes sent me a small bottle of pink medicine for my dolls as well as what he had prescribed for me. My medicine tasted dreadful, but no matter how much fuss I made Mother still insisted that I must swallow it. 'Open your shoulders and let it run down,' she instructed me. As well as bringing the medicine Father often bought fruit for me in town, peaches and pears as a special treat. Mother made beef tea to aid my recovery. In the evenings Father came to sit on my bed. He was never any good at reading aloud, that was Mother's job, but he could draw quite beautifully. He took his black fountain pen out of his pocket and with it he drew spidery windmills, always with cats sitting in the foreground; and he drew birds, blackbirds with big eyes, and herons, 'old hansers' as he called them, with long thin feet. Sometimes Mother sent Skinny to read to me. She chose lurid stories, no doubt on purpose to terrify me so that she would not be given the job again. She liked reading a story about a man being attacked by a black panther. After hearing it I used to wake in the night, screaming, convinced that the black panther was in my bedroom.

When Mother came to entertain me she usually read aloud, but occasionally she could be persuaded to recount the story of 'Pepper and

Salt'. There was once a poor woodcutter who had two children, a boy called Pepper and a girl called Salt, Mother told us. When his first wife died the woodcutter remarried and the children acquired a wicked stepmother. She hated the children and one day, whilst the father was out cutting wood, she decided to make away with Pepper. She killed him and cut up his body and cooked it in a big stewpot. After it was cooked, poor Salt, who was absolutely terrified, had to perform the gruesome task of picking all the meat off the bones. She was then forced to lay the bones out on the stone flags in the back yard to await their burial by the wicked stepmother. That evening, when the father came home from his work, the stepmother gave him the meat for his supper, and Salt was much too frightened to tell him what he was eating. When the woodcutter had finished his meal they heard a tiny sighing voice coming from the yard where the bones lay. 'My mother killed me, my father ate me, my little sister picked my bones and laid them on the cold marble stones.' 'What was that?' asked the father. 'Oh, that's only the wind sighing in the trees,' his wife told him. 'Where is Pepper?' asked the woodcutter, and the wicked stepmother replied that she had sent the boy out on an errand. Then the voice came again, eerie and quavering, but louder this time, 'My mother killed me, my father ate me, my little sister picked my bones, and laid them on the cold marble stones.' At this Salt began to cry. 'Poor Pepper! Poor Pepper!' she sobbed. Then the father found out what the wicked stepmother had done and he was so angry that he seized his wood chopper and cut off her head. I never tired of hearing this fantastic story, although it frightened me. I used to lie awake and listen to the sounds outside in the garden. Sometimes the wind made a lot of noise in the trees, and I would call Mother for comfort. 'You don't want to worry,' she reassured me. 'That's only the Dippy a-roaring.'

The one and only time I remember Father being ill was when he had whooping cough. Just after Christmas one year, Mother's youngest sister came to stay, bringing her small son with her, and he caught whooping cough. Of course we children all got it, and then Father did too. He was outraged, and swore against my aunt for bringing the little boy into the house. Poor Father was really ill, and he coughed and coughed. He looked terrible and made as much fuss as possible. He got depressed. The only food he felt he could fancy was a dish of oysters, so Mother had to make complicated arrangements to get fresh oysters brought to the town daily. Every afternoon Skinny and I, now convalescent, walked the two miles across the causeway to the town and back, to collect them for Father. The wind was blisteringly cold as only an East Anglian north-east wind can be, cutting straight across the marshes, but I suppose it was good for whooping cough, and all that fresh air contributed to my speedy recovery; anyway, I was not ill for long. Father was not so lucky. As he began to get better he used to crawl off to bed in the early evening out of boredom rather than exhaustion. He never failed to tell Mother how ill he felt. Then one evening an old crony of his came to see him and, although Father had just gone upstairs to bed, he came rushing down again when he heard his visitor's voice in the hall. The two men sat in the wireless room drinking whisky and laughing until the small hours. Mother was outraged. She said it proved Father had not been really ill at all, and he had just been making her life difficult for nothing. She said he complained when his little finger ached and that many a time she had been forced to keep about when she had not known how to hold her head up. So they had another good row and Father's recovery was established.

Although Mother did not have any sympathy for Father when he was ill, she did have a lot for Uncle Bernie. He had a very pronounced limp, having had one knee smashed by a cricket ball when he was a boy, and he walked with the help of a stick. For Mother this made him an object of pity, and she revelled in it. Father hardly managed to tolerate Uncle Bernie; he certainly did not like him. 'Bloody lame duck,' Father called him, in moments of exasperation, but never to his face. When Mother fussed round Uncle Bernie Father said, 'You don't pay no regard to anyone what haven't got nothing the matter with them; you always did like a lame duck.' For a long time I thought that the term 'lame duck' simply referred to Uncle Bernie's lame leg, but in the end I found out that Father regarded him as a hopeless failure and meant it in that sense too. Everything Uncle Bernie undertook failed. He was a languishing hero who looked pale and interesting, at any rate to Mother. Fate had kicked Uncle Bernie around. Father scorned him. If Fate had kicked Father he would have kicked back and shown it who could kick hardest. He made it quite clear to us that he thought any other attitude faint-hearted.

When Uncle Bernie was not having migraines, he worked in his youth as an electrician at Windsor Castle. He gave us wonderful descriptions of how he had to arrange the lighting for state banquets. Once when he was on duty he hid in a passage doorway to watch the royal party going in to dinner. The king, who was Edward VII, noticed someone lurking in the shadows and commanded Bernie to come out and show himself. Then he asked Bernie what he was doing, and when he heard that it was Bernie's job to keep the electricity functioning in the castle he said, 'Well, see that the lights don't go out during dinner, young man!' and swept on his way, the Queen of Portugal on his arm, followed by the King of Portugal with Queen Alexandra. Mother thought this story most glamorous. She was a fervent royalist, but Father always held that Oliver Cromwell was one of the few characters in history who knew what he was about. Mother told us that while Uncle Bernie was at Windsor he used to go up to London and talk to prostitutes. (I did not know what prostitutes were, but Skinny did; she had read about them in the Bible.) When asked, Mother replied that she did not know what he talked to them about. It never occurred to her that the prostitutes might have been justifiably angry with him for wasting their time. Mother told us that Uncle Bernie said we all ought to be grateful to prostitutes because if they did not exist to do their job it would not be safe for decent women and girls to go about alone. This advice impressed Mother a good deal. She thought it showed that Uncle Bernie was an experienced man of the world who knew all about city life.

Mother said Uncle Bernie was a ladies' man and clearly she thought him wonderful, so there was great excitement when he talked of getting married. He appeared to have a formidable choice of candidates. Stories of girls queuing up for him and getting their hearts broken filtered through to us children in carefully dropped hints. We understood that he had considered proposing to Mother at one time, but what would she have wanted with a penniless electrician? Bernie's elder brother Horace had actually proposed to Mother. He had been in love with her before he was killed in the 1914-18 war. She liked to tell us about him, and how romantic he was. 'Poor Horace,' she said smugly, 'I could have had him if I'd liked,' and she showed us a faded photograph of him in his army uniform, which she kept in her jewel case. Father derided Mother's memories of Horace, and seemed to think him the bigger fool for getting killed. He was certain that going to fight in the war was a fool's errand, and managed to dodge going himself. Flour milling was a reserved occupation in that war, it seems, but if it had not been Father would have found a way of making it so. 'Them what went into the army expected to be buggered about,' he said.

Mother loved to tell us tales about the war. My two sisters had been little children then, before I was born. Mother said that when the Zepps came over Father never stayed indoors with his wife and children as he ought to have done, to comfort them in their hour of danger; instead he put on his hat and went rushing out round the mill. He never came into the house again until the raid was over, but stayed outside to keep watch that his beloved mill should not come to harm. Father felt that if he was about the place no Zepp would dare to come too near, let alone drop a bomb on his property. If he had been asked to choose between the mill and his family getting blown up, it was clear what his choice would have been. He would not have hesitated to save his business.

Finally all speculation on Bernie's marriage prospects was ended abruptly when he announced that he had got a wife and was bringing her to stay at the Mill House. Mother did not seem delighted by the news. Uncle Bernie's wife was called Dulcie; she was very tall and angular with a cloche hat pulled down over fashionably shingled hair, pointed crocodile-skin strap shoes and a coat with an immense amount of fur round the neck and cuffs, but she was not pretty, certainly not pretty. She finished off her shingle with a little wavy fringe which really belonged to an earlier style, and which we considered rather old-fashioned. It made her horsy face look more doleful than ever. She was very flat-chested, in contrast to Mother, who was busty and well-covered. When the pair arrived, Uncle Bernie hurried out to do a bit of fishing in the mill pond; he felt safer out of doors, and the ladies settled down for a good long heart-to-heart talk in the drawing room. Dulcie told Mother how she had managed to get Bernie to marry her. He had shilly-shallied, she said, but she forced him to make the decision; he had fooled about long enough. Mother obviously felt a bit sorry for Uncle Bernie, although she could not admit it. Women had

to stick together whatever happened, but Mother did go rather quiet and tight-lipped when she heard Dulcie's story.

Uncle Teddie did not like Uncle Bernie any better than Father did, as Mother well knew, but she was determined that the two of them should help entertain the visitors, and she persuaded Father and Uncle Bernie to take the guests out with them when they went to markets, and on 'short rounds'. On one trip to Norwich Uncle Bernie was such a nuisance that they decided to teach the old windbag a lesson so that he would not want to come out with them again. Coming home, they invited Bernie to sit in the back of the car with Dulcie while Father and Uncle Teddie rode in front. They planned to drive fast enough to give Uncle Bernie a good fright and a shaking up, so as they approached the humped back bridge at Woolton Father accelerated, and the car flew off the top of the bridge and came down on the far side with a terrible crash. This was a little more dramatic than anything they had intended, and when Father had got the car under control again he looked back to see how his passengers had fared. Father's car was a big one, with space for two fold-up seats behind the front seat, as well as having an ample back seat where Bernie and Dulcie had been sitting. They had fallen into the wide floor space, and lay on their backs with their legs hopelessly entwined. 'Why Bernie,' Father said reprovingly, 'can't you two newly-weds wait 'till you get home?' This remark delighted Uncle Teddie, but not Uncle Bernie, who was unconscious, bleeding from a cut on his head where he had hit the roof of the car. They stopped and revived him as best they could, then hurried home, somewhat crestfallen at the thought of facing Mother. When Bernie was helped into the kitchen Mother was horrified. She administered brandy, bandaged his head and got him into bed. Then she started to ask how the accident had happened. Dulcie went upstairs to sit with her wounded husband, and Uncle Teddie escaped out of the door into the garden, but Mother got the truth out of Father and gave him a piece of her mind. Father was not penitent. He said he reckoned he had 'done a conjure' and 'that served the silly old bugger right.'

After Uncle Bernie married and had left his job as an electrician at Windsor, he tried his hand at various white-collar jobs around the outskirts of London. He and Dulcie lived in a depressing series of drab flats. At one time he was manager of a cinema in Middlesex. This was the era of silent films, and when we went to visit I was taken behind the cinema screen and told not make a noise or the audience would hear it. Although there was always music for an accompaniment to the films, it was Uncle Bernie's ambition to improve on it with something more realistic. He collected all sorts of objects with which to make his sound effects, whistles and strange devices, and with these he made what he thought were appropriate noises during the performances. I was allowed to help. He used to make the MGM lion roar even in those silent days. Living in reduced circumstances in an urban district was not good for Dulcie's health. Sometimes square meals were scarce, and life was altogether rather threadbare. As a girl she had spent a long time in a sanatorium. Mother said Dulcie was consumptive, and that Uncle Bernie had known when he married her that she was almost certain to return to the sanatorium and die there. In those days anyone who had consumption always died of it sooner or later. There was no cure, but life was prolonged by huge doses of fresh air, and the victims lived outdoors in huts, open to freezing weather, or on hospital balconies exposed to tearing winds. Sure enough, after a few years Dulcie did go back to the sanatorium, and Uncle Bernie visited her every day until she died. In Father's opinion Dulcie's illness and death were evidence of yet another failure on Uncle Bernie's part. 'Seeing he picked a dud,' Father pronounced, 'I don't know what more he expect!'

Although Uncle Bernie was the only family friend who came to stay with us, there were plenty of local people who came to the house. Mother's friends were strictly divided from Father's except in the case of one family, the Bedwells. Sonny Bedwell was Father's crony, but Mother accepted Mrs Bedwell as being what she called 'a nice little woman'. There were two bouncing farmer sons and a very pretty daughter, Mollie, who was a little older than Skinny. In later years, when Mollie got married, Father and Sonny Bedwell both attended the service in the village church, which so surprised the parson that he said that if ever those two men entered the church together a second time the tower would fall down. Father remembered this insult and waited to get his own back on the parson. He never forgot the smallest slight and would bide his time for years if necessary; it was worth having patience because he always won in the end. In this instance he had to wait until he got on Lacton Town Council, and the question of allowing the local cinema to open on Sundays came to a vote. The parson called to see Father and asked him to vote against Sunday films, but Father refused. 'If the church can't stand a little healthy competition,' he said, 'I reckon that's time that went out of business.' After that the cinema opened seven days a week.

Every Christmas we were all invited to the Bedwell's house. We were not offered one of Mother's polite teas, but a huge farm tea, and the big table was laden with unimaginable delicacies. There was a beautiful big glass bowl of fruit salad, and with the fruit Mrs Bedwell offered bread and butter. 'I'm afraid my children won't eat bread and butter with fruit,' Mother said, preening herself. Wholesome, plain food was the fashion for children then, even amongst those who had plenty of money for housekeeping, and you did not expect to get jam and butter on the same slice of bread, but Mother never believed in such methods, and we always had grown-up food at home, even cream if it was going. She felt it showed that we had been brought up lavishly if we were not accustomed to spin out our fruit with bread and butter. It made us a cut above the Bedwells, which was only right and proper,

as they were working farmers, not gentlemen farmers, when all was said and done.

Father used to buy little pigs from Sonny Bedwell, and fatten them up for market. He always had plenty of pig food from the mill, and it became a good sideline for him. Sonny was a wicked, foxy-faced old devil, with sandy hair and a florid complexion, this last probably due to over-indulgence in the pub on market days. He wore buskins. Most local people whom we knew wore them, and Father had two pairs, a brown and a black to go with his boots. He never wore the brown ones; perhaps they had belonged to Grand-dad in the days when he had two legs; certainly Father would never have bought brown ones for himself. Sonny Bedwell rarely came into the house. He and Father had long conversations hanging over the wall of the pig sty together. When Sonny did come indoors he and Father retired to the wireless room to drink whisky and laugh. Mother thought it was all rather low, and said it was not very edifying. Once, when Sonny delivered a batch of piglets, Father decided to give one to me. We spent some time watching the newly-arrived piglets running round in their sty, trying to decide which one was mine, but they all looked alike. Father said my pig could live with the others and that he would provide its food; when it was fat enough for market I could have the money which he got for it. This was clear profit for me, and I was delighted. After the first pig was sold and Father paid me, I was able to buy another. I was in business, and I could not lose. Later, when I had saved a bit, I bought two pigs. Father decided that I would not be allowed to have more than two pigs at a time. He was not going to feed a full sty for me, but nevertheless I was proud of my pig money.

Mother did not disapprove of Sonny Bedwell so much as some of Father's friends; the one she loathed was old Wally Love. He was a shady milling character with a huge family, all sons. He used to meet Father in Norwich market and sometimes came to visit in the evenings when the two would put through doubtful deals over many glasses of whisky. Wally often stayed very late, and Mother disapproved of that too. There was another old friend of Father's, a sad little character whom we knew as Uncle Arthur. He was the brother of a great friend of Father's who had emigrated to Johannesburg, and when he went Father took up with Uncle Arthur in place of him. Uncle Arthur lived and worked in Lacton. He bicycled over to the Mill House on Sunday mornings, and he and Father took a glass of something together. When I was old enough to go to church, and Father's Sunday mornings were his own again, he liked to spend them catching up on all the local gossip with Uncle Arthur. Mother would discover them drinking and what she called scandalmongering when she came home from church. Uncle Arthur never stayed for Sunday lunch; he was not invited. 'The man ought to get home to his wife,' Mother said. The wife was a mousy little creature whom we knew only as Mrs White, not any sort of Auntie. She had thick pebble spectacles and a nervous tinkling laugh, and she seemed unable to raise her head when she spoke. At long intervals Mother asked Uncle Arthur and Mrs White to Sunday tea in the drawing room, with lace doilies on the plates. They came riding demurely on their bicycles. We were never invited to their house at all. Father and I passed it every time we went to fetch Aunt Eliza from Lacton mill. Father pointed it out. 'That's Uncle Arthur's house,' he said, 'the one with the monkey puzzle tree.' It was a small terrace house and the tree in the little square of front garden was its only distinguishing mark. Father drove past without stopping the car so the interior of Uncle Arthur's and Mrs White's house remained a mystery to me.

Sunday tea with visitors, or indeed any of Mother's tea parties, were a special form of torture to the household. Each day, when Mother was at home, she never failed to break off what she was doing in the middle of the afternoon and go to wash and change her dress so that she would look nice in case anyone called. When visitors were known to be coming she used to change a bit earlier and hurry downstairs again to cut sandwiches. She was a poor hand with the saw-edged bread knife. Father had never managed to teach her to use it satisfactorily, so she cut the bread and butter with the carver. The result was that the knife was always blunt when required for carving the joint. Father accused her of cutting bread with it, and a row followed.

Another pitfall of having visitors was the drawing room fire. This fire was hardly ever lit as on most days the room was only used by Mother for playing the piano, which she did happily enough in the cold. The fireplace had a wicked little grate, flat on the hearth with no draught at all. Only Mother could light that fire, and even she had difficulty in getting it going and keeping it from fading out before the guests arrived. Strong measures were called for, and the maid was ordered to bring more sticks while Mother got down on her hands and knees to grapple with that fire. Mother forbade anyone to touch it when she had got it alight. Skinny had once successfully blacked it out with a hodful of coal just before some important person put in an appearance, and Mother was not likely to forget that incident in a hurry. For me the drawing room was totally out of bounds, and with good reason. Once, when tea was laid out ready for the visitors, I kicked the cake stand, causing its three tiers to fold, cakes and all, as it crashed to the ground. On the rare occasions when Mother felt unable to exclude me from the drawing room, she kept an eagle eye on me and never stopped telling me to sit still. I hated that room, and have since wondered if Mother's friends disliked it too. It was scarcely welcoming, decorated in cold pale mauves, and it smelt rather damp in there. Portrait photographs of us children from the age of six months onwards were hung around the walls. There was Skinny as a baby sitting bare-toed on a fur rug and holding an artificial rose, and

Mother's favourite picture, Skinny and Milly together aged about six or seven, wearing long white crochet socks and white smocks, their hair arranged in careful ringlets. I thought that some of the photographs of myself were fearful. The stiff unused atmosphere and air of gentility which pervaded the room were carefully preserved by Mother. The moment her visitors had gone she removed all traces of their presence, plumped up the cushions, had the maid sweep up the crumbs, and pulled the curtains across the window again to keep the sunlight from fading the carpet. It was Mother's drawing room, and that was the way she liked to keep it.

VII

Mother did not have any close friends in the village but she had a large circle of acquaintances. She was not on first-name terms with any of them. In the village a very strict social order was observed; every family knew its place and was expected to remain in it. At the top were the people who lived in the Hall. This was a vast, rambling, red-brick pile situated in an isolated position well outside the village, and was let, with all its grounds and shooting estate, to an elderly couple, the Warrens. Nobody that we knew had ever seen either of them. It was said that the lady was an invalid, and that Mr Warren had a lot of shooting parties. Beyond that they were a mystery. The couple had an obscure relative living with them who was their only contact with the village. She was Miss Holmes, a very lively well-dressed American lady whose exact position in the Warren household remained unknown. Every Sunday morning Miss Holmes came to matins, driven to the church by the Hall chauffeur, in the Hall car, and sat in the Hall pew, a high-sided horse-box affair with a black fur rug on the floor. We could see the top of her hat over the wooden side of the pew, but that was all. As soon as the service was over she got into the car and was whisked away again. It was Miss Holmes's duty to preside at every village function. She made her little speech on behalf of the Warrens, saying how disappointed Mrs Warren was that she was unable to be present on that happy occasion. She then called for a round of applause, so loud that it could be heard by Mrs Warren in her room at the Hall, to show appreciation for her support, prizes for the Sunday school, or money for the church funds; after which Miss Holmes retired gracefully to the Hall again.

We were all expected to help decorate the church for festivals, Christmas, Easter, and Harvest Thanksgiving, and in this Miss Holmes played her rightful part. Here, as elsewhere, the village hierarchy was strictly adhered to and Miss Holmes stood at the altar filling the big brass vases (which someone else had cleaned) with arum lilies from the Hall greenhouses. Mother had the choir stalls to decorate, the parson's wife did the lectern, and the head gardener from the Hall got the font. The pulpit was left alone as it was so beautifully carved that it seemed a shame to cover it up. Lesser mortals were assigned a window ledge to decorate. The ledges all sloped, and pumpkins, apples, marrows and jars of flowers placed there readily cascaded to the floor and rolled amongst the pews. It was no job for the unwary. The lowliest helpers had to fill jam jars with water, and were told to sweep up the leaves on the floor. This was my task and I was engaged on it when I met Miss Holmes in the church. Everyone seemed much in awe of her, but I liked her, and she always spoke to me. One Christmas, after she had finished her altar vases she came to help me hang whole branches of greenery from the balcony at the back of the church. We had enormous fun fixing them there and everyone else was most surprised at this unlikely bit of co-operation.

Mother was quite a pillar of the church, or thought she ought to be one. Apart from festivals, five ladies took it in turns to do the church flowers. Mother had the second Sunday in every month for her turn, while the parson's wife got the fifth. 'You can see who come off best,' Mother said. 'There aren't many months what have five Sundays.' While I was quite small Mother often took me with her when she went to do the altar flowers. I was left to wander round the church while she worked. For some reason I was convinced that Jesus was buried under the altar. I did not tell anyone, but one day when Mother's back was turned I peeped under the altar cloth just to make sure and saw only table legs and the stone-flagged floor: no grave, no tomb. It was a terrible let-down and I was glad I had kept my belief to myself so that no one could laugh at my mistake.

All the village knew that the Hall was leased to the Warrens because the owner, the present young squire, was too poor to maintain it. He was rarely seen in the village as he was in the army and usually stationed overseas. The story was that the old squire, his father, had owned large estates in Ireland as well as in Norfolk. Every six months or so he told his wife that it was time he went to look after his Irish property. She was required to remain in England to keep an eye on the Norfolk estate and take care of the children. This was accepted as perfectly reasonable by everyone concerned and the arrangement went on for years, with the old squire spending half his time in Ireland and half in England. When he was an old man and his sons were grown up, the squire made his final visit to Ireland where he died of a sudden illness. He had expressed a wish to be buried in England in the family vault and, as was expected, arrangements were made to transport his body back to Norfolk. Unknown to everyone, the old squire had kept a second wife and family in Ireland and it was believed that his guilty secret was not discovered until the sons from Norfolk going to meet their father's body and the sons from Ireland escorting that same body met on a train somewhere between Holyhead and Tivetshall. It was a good story, but scarcely likely that, even in those times of difficult travel and poor communications, it could have been possible for the old squire to keep up his deception so successfully. However, many people considered that the maintenance of the two families had been the cause of the present impoverished conditions on the estates. The properties were entailed and had been inherited by the eldest English son, the present young squire. It was impossible for him to sell off any of the land to meet his debts, so he had to make the best of a bad job by renting out what he could.

The Lodge, also the squire's property, was leased as well, and a rather mysterious family, the Dixons, lived there. Mrs Dixon used to come to take tea with Mother. If it was a hot afternoon she would flop down on the sofa, her frail braceleted arms flung out along the back of it, and gasp, 'My dear! It's Colombo heat!' It was understood that her husband was in Ceylon and she visited him there once a year for a few months. We never saw Mr Dixon. There was no flying backwards and forwards then, so Mrs Dixon went out and back by boat, leaving her two pretty daughters at boarding school in England. When she was not in Ceylon or on a boat coming or going, Mrs Dixon stayed at the Lodge, and the girls came there for their school holidays. The idea of wives and children commuting to the east by air was then a thing of the future, and all the families whose fathers worked in India and Ceylon were split up as the Dixons were. The wives, like Mrs Dixon, had a dreadful life, torn between husband and children, and it must have been hard for every member of such a family, even though it was their accepted way of life.

After the Hall and the Lodge, but well below them in the village hierarchy, came the Vicarage. It was a huge house, and the family was a jolly one. There were two girls a little older than my sisters, and a nearly grown-up son. The living was a poor one and Mother said she

77

was sure they did not have enough money. When she was helping to price the jumble sale items she noticed that, in the bundle from the Vicarage, all the underclothes had been mended. She said that she had thought it best not to pass any remark at the time. We nicknamed the parson's wife Lally, but of course we never called her that to her face. She was Mrs Snead. Being the parson's wife, Lally had to attend every church service, and she did so wearing a brown felt hat with a brown veil covering her face. She sat in the pew directly in front of ours and I had a good view of her as she dutifully sang all the hymns and psalms. The veil used to go up and down, in and out, as it stretched over her very white double chin. Lally's Vicarage was a lovely spacious house with the most splendid lavatory I had ever seen. It was a water closet, which was no mean achievement for a country Vicarage. The room was a large one; presumably it had once been one of the smaller bedrooms, perhaps a dressing room at an earlier date. One side of the room under the high window was entirely filled with a gigantic mahogany seat. Two steps, also mahogany, and highly polished, reached up to this throne. In the middle of the seat was a hole containing a beautiful lavatory pan, decorated with a pattern of blue flowers. The long chain which I had to pull to flush the lavatory hung far back, and luckily well to one side, as I had to climb up and stand on the seat to reach it. I used to keep asking to go to that lavatory because I enjoyed it so much.

When Lally's son Max was a little boy he had a big teddy bear called Buster. I had a book which Max's uncle had written about Buster's adventures. It was a lovely story and I never tired of having it read to me and looking at the pictures. It told how one evening, after the children had gone to bed, Buster sat alone in front of the dying fire in the nursery. He could see castles and landscapes in the glowing fire, and as he watched he fell asleep. In his dream he walked in the embers and had all kinds of adventures in the castles. When morning came he knew that his experiences had not been just a dream because his socks were twisted and wrinkled from so much walking. Although Max was grown up now, he had still kept Buster. If I looked up from the Vicarage garden, I could see the bear sitting, wearing his socks, on the window sill of Max's bedroom. He looked down at me with a kindly, beady gaze, and I felt very fond of him.

The Mill House was known to come below the Vicarage in the

social scale, but no one could quite assess the correct position of the Laurels. The house belonged to the two Miss Randalls. To us they seemed very old indeed. They had very little money because they had given all their savings to the Waifs and Strays Society, Miss Edith's pet charity, indeed her total obsession. The Laurels was surrounded by tangled, dripping evergreens, and one had to struggle through a bent and rusting wrought iron gate in the wall under the trees to reach the front door, dark under its heavy verandah. Inside the house there was a clutter of Victorian furniture and ornaments, not fashionable then, just old-fashioned, and there was a smell of mustiness and unwashed old ladies. The windows were never opened and the sun had given up trying to penetrate into the house and garden. Miss Emily, the younger of the two sisters, played the organ in church. The organ had to be pumped by one of the choir boys. If he forgot to pump there was no wind to begin the hymns and the organ let out an angry sneeze when she struck the first note, which agitated Miss Emily considerably. We could see the top of her hat twitching about above the rather grubby yellow curtain which served as an organ screen. Miss Edith, the elder sister, was small and bent and the possessor of a dark moustache. She wore little round steel-rimmed spectacles and scraped back her sparse grey hair into a tight bun under her hat. She rode into the town on a vintage tricycle, painted black. Miss Edith crossing the causeway from Lacton on a wet and blowy afternoon in mid-winter was an unforgettable sight. In the gloaming, as she breasted the last hump-backed bridge, she appeared as if from nowhere, a tiny black figure with flapping cloak, pedalling madly with head bent into the wind, trying to get home before lighting-up time. Both ladies were always seen in black button boots, long grey skirts, and with their black hats securely anchored on their grey hair by long silver hat pins. The hats were worn absolutely straight; the sisters were not inclined to compromise. We children rarely visited the Laurels. Sometimes I was taken there by Mother to a Women's Institute meeting, or we went to bazaars in the garden, in aid of the Waifs and Strays. It was always very dark, and Miss Edith gave a little talk explaining how needy the Waifs and Strays Society was, but she spoke so softly that no one could hear her.

Being a milling family we were trade, not gentry, but in those hungry days Father was considered wealthy and had a lot of influence locally. He owned nearly half the cottages in the village. It had been Grand-dad's policy to house his own workmen, the better to make them toe the line. If he lived in a tied cottage a man was unlikely to risk dismissal, but also it was almost impossible to take on fresh labour unless a house was available. There were no council houses near us, but in any case they were considered rather a low form of accommodation. A good workman expected something better than that. Father's houses were by far the best maintained in the village, and he kept up the standard, eventually installing electricity in all of them, and even indoor sanitation where it was possible. Every time a good cottage came on the market Father bought it, and he and Mother went to look over it and see what needed to be done to improve it. Often I went with them and was left to wander in and out of the empty rooms while my parents discussed plans. Most of the rooms were tiny, with little closely-shut windows and flowered wallpaper. A door in the kitchen opened on to a steep winding staircase, so narrow that bedroom furniture could not be carried up it. On moving day one of the bedroom windows was taken out and the furniture hoisted through the gap, but even so a double bed would have to be cut in half and bolted together again when it was in position. Downstairs there were only two rooms, the kitchen and the front room. The front door opened directly into the front room, and was usually nailed up against draughts. This scarcely mattered as the front room was hardly ever used. Everyone went round the back and the family lived in the kitchen with its black range to keep them warm. Every drop of hot water was heated on that kitchen range, except when the copper was lighted for wash day or bath night, and all the family's meals were cooked on it too. In every room the wooden floors were cleanly scrubbed by the outgoing tenant and they smelled sweet and rang hollow under my feet, while I danced about waiting for Father and Mother. As soon as word got round the village that Father had bought a fresh cottage, the workmen's wives started coming to Mother to appeal for a chance to move into better accommodation, while all the millers and other employees were busy putting in a good word with Father. They always got it sorted out in the end. Father appeared to be scrupulously fair in giving the best houses to the best and longest-standing of his men, but this was an easy matter as these were naturally his favourites in any case. He loaned them a mill lorry to transport their furniture when they moved to a better house; he lent it on a Saturday afternoon, and they got their friends to give a hand lifting things and laying lino, so they were never out of pocket over the move.

The husband of one family always spent the rent money in the pub. He was a good miller and one of Father's favourites, so he was allowed a little leeway in respect of the rent until things had gone too far. Then the wife, who had been my sisters' nursemaid, came to the back door of our house to borrow the money from Mother so that her husband could take it across the yard to the office to settle up with Father. Mother was often made use of in that sort of way. In the early 1930s, if you were so ill that you had to be taken to hospital, you were considered finished. People went to hospital to die, the villagers maintained, and more often than not this was proved to be correct. The local convent hospital ran a contributory scheme for poor families. They paid two pence each week, and Mother took on the job of collecting the hospital money for the village. It turned out that she had to find the money for several of the participants herself, but the scheme was considered very advanced and everybody said what a good idea it was. If a family had paid its contributions then any member of it was entitled to go into hospital free if the need arose. Two pence a week was a lot of money then and it was not surprising that many people fell behind with their payments, for one reason or another. Sure enough, those would be the very ones who would need to have a son or daughter admitted to the hospital. Then the wife would come to see Mother and promise tearfully never to let the contributions lapse again if she could be helped just that once. Mother always produced the necessary money, but she was so sanctimonious about it that she must have made the unfortunate women feel very resentful. None of Father's employees dare fail to take part in the scheme while Mother ran it.

As well as being responsible for the hospital contributory scheme, Mother looked after the baby-weighing. One afternoon in each month village women who had young babies brought them to the Hut, as the Village Hall was called, to be weighed and checked by the District Nurse. Mother always attended, and sometimes she took me with her.

81

There was very little heating in the Hut and as the babies were always weighed naked my job was to go round closing all the windows to get some warmth into the room before the nurse arrived. She brought the weighing machine with her. Someone looked out of the window and said, 'Here come the nurse,' as she staggered along with her load. There was a big metal dish, with a piece of flannel in it for the babies to lie on whilst the nurse lifted brass weights off and on the other side of the scales. Some of the babies howled at this indignity, but baby-weighing was popular with the women. It gave them a chance to show off their babies and have a chat with the other mothers, or get advice from the nurse. After the weighing there was always tea, with buns in paper cases. Mother was very deferential to the nurse, but she was proud of her village babies. Nurse told her that she found most of the babies in 'good plight', and the mothers seemed nicely too, so that was a feather in Mother's cap. She was put out if any of the mothers and babies failed to attend, especially if they were the wives and children of Father's men.

Father's workmen had some standing in the village. Although they were considered beneath the Hall gamekeepers, chauffeur and indoor staff, they were definitely a cut above the farm labourers, and their daughters went into service in big houses like the Hall, where they got proper training. Mother had to recruit her endless stream of maids from the farm labouring families in the village. Those were the days when the servant lived in the kitchen, and when it was not her evening out she sat in the black horsehair chair beside the old kitchen range, mending her stockings or making a rag rug. Mother kept two maids when she could and they slept in the two bedrooms above the kitchen and larder, which were reached by a steep back staircase through a door in the kitchen wall. We children were never allowed to go up those back stairs. Mother's maids did not stay with her for long. Either they rebelled at her fussy ways and left to get other jobs, or else left pregnant to get married. The local women thought that the Mill House offered a good place for their daughters who had to go into service. The bedrooms were reasonably comfortable, and as they had no bathroom at home they did not miss it, nor object to using a tin bath once a week, sharing our family bathroom being quite out of the question. The food was good and plentiful, and Mother gave the girls a rigid training. Very often they grew plump and rosy in our house, and did not seem unhappy. As well as the two maids, Mother employed a 'woman' who came in to do the scrubbing. She was a lovely, kind person, in a flowered pinarette which was stretched to bursting point over her ample bosom and huge behind. Over the pinarette she wore a large, clean blue apron, and over that again a thick sacking one in which she could kneel without getting her legs too wet. Always her sleeves were rolled up showing immensely fat white arms, and always she was on her knees scrubbing. I scarcely remember seeing her standing up.

In spite of having so much help in the house, Mother's work was seemingly never done. She said she had to 'see after things' herself: there were so many jobs she could never trust anyone else to do properly. When a room was to be cleaned it had to be cleared of all ornaments lest the maid break one. Newspapers were folded up neatly; cushions and antimacassars were continually being straightened. Mother did not like to see anything left about, she said. Curtains were washed often, and bedspreads too. Usually the latter were white with crochet, lace or hemstitched borders. No washing was done at home except the maids' underclothes, dusters, and Mother's best stockings. The rest was divided into two groups. Good things needing starching or 'getting up' went to the laundry and had to be marked. These included Father's stiff collars, seven each week. Mother always listed each item carefully herself in the green laundry book, before packing everything in a basket hamper with leather straps, ready for the laundry man's call. When the hamper was returned she checked the list again just as carefully and raised hell if any item was missing or imperfectly laundered. The second best things to be washed went in another basket to 'the woman'. Amongst these were Father's socks, seven navy-blue pairs each week. This basket hamper was collected by a small jolly lorry-driver whom we nicknamed Goggles, because he had rather bulging eyes. He dropped the basket of dirty washing off at the woman's cottage when he passed by with his loaded lorry from the mill, and picked up the previous week's clean laundry in exchange. He did that every Friday. There was always a rush to get the dirty washing ready in time before he called for it, just after breakfast. In later years Goggles used to come to take Milly's school trunk to the station. When he came into the house he always took off his cap. Then I saw that the

83

lower part of his face was brown while the top part was revealed as white, and this fascinated me. He carried the trunk down the stairs on his back, like a sack of corn. He was one of the men who had originally worked for Grand-dad. When the old man died Goggles agreed to stay a week with Father as his new boss, to see if he liked it. He did not expect to like it, but he must have done because he stayed on for forty years.

The whole of the village life centred round the church and the Women's Institute. The village school was a church school, and Mother was one of the managers. I remember one boy getting a scholarship from there to the local grammar school. It was a tremendous event. All the other children went through the village school's two classrooms and left for work when they were fourteen years old. Most gatherings of importance took place in the school because there was more space there than in the Hut. There was a small room for infants and a big room for the rest. That was all. The privies were across the iron-railed playground. The Christmas Sunday School treat was held in the school. Mother used to take us along to help, although we never went to Sunday School. There were pounds and pounds of cheap boiled sweets to be sorted and bagged up so that each child got its correct share. The sweets went into little, white, three-cornered bags supplied by the village shop. We were forbidden to eat the sweets while we were parcelling them up, but if any were left over the parson's wife, Lally, let me take them. I adored those boiled sweets. Mother would never have allowed us to buy them from the big jars in the village shop because they were cheap and, she suspected, none too clean. She doled out plain, wholesome, individually-wrapped Mackintosh's toffees to her children. The boiled sweets came in lovely colours; the best were pear-shaped, one side red and one side yellow. When I was given the left-over sweets I looked immediately, with some anxiety, to see how many, if any, of this sort my bag contained. After we had dealt with the sweets we had to wrap and label a present for each child, and these were hung on the Christmas tree. There was much discussion amongst the lady helpers as to the suitability of each toy for each respective child. Early in December Mother and Lally had an expedition to Norwich where the nearest Woolworth's was, to buy all the presents. Everything in 'Woollies' was priced at sixpence or less, and they got

some very good things. The huge Christmas tree was supplied by the Hall, as was all the cash for the sweets, presents, tea and prizes. These last were given for attendance at Sunday School, not for actually learning anything.

Decorating the tree was fun because it meant using a step-ladder. The parson's wife ran round giving orders and then changing her mind. On the night of the treat we all turned up, I in my velvet dress with its white lace collar, and the parson's grown-up son Max dressed as Father Christmas, ready to give away the presents from the tree. First came the tea. We had to pass round plates of bread and butter and bread and jam. Not until this was all eaten were we permitted to take round plates of cake. It was shop slab cake cut in wedges, full of fruit and absolutely delicious. We never had cake like that at home as Mother considered it inferior to her own baking, but I always hoped that there would be some left over so that I could get a piece. The children ate like wolves, but their manners were perfect. Remembering the sparse diet of the village families in those days, it must have been a very tempting feast for them, but no one grabbed at the plate I offered, nor tried to take two pieces of cake at once. I never questioned what they thought of me, dressed up in my velvet.

VIII

Father did not go into an ordinary shop to buy anything if he could avoid doing so. He liked to drive into Lacton, stop his big car outside a shop and sound the horn. Then the shopkeeper would come running out, full of humble zeal, and Father talked to him through the car window. Goods were brought out for his inspection, and sometimes Father made a purchase. Then the article was wrapped up and brought out by a shop assistant, who put it into the car. No money changed hands; bills were sent in later. One shop Father did enter was the dark little tailor's establishment in Lacton. The proprietor made all Father's suits, and they were all made to exactly the same design, only the cloth varied from winter to summer weight, and from one shade of grey to another. All Father's clothes came from Lacton, even his boots and knitted silk ties. He had to go into the tailor's shop from time to time to be remeasured as he grew plumper in middle age. Sometimes he brought home a swatch of patterns which he thumbed through. Then he asked Mother's advice, and finally decided on the same cloth as he had chosen for the previous suit. Father's shopping for clothes was a necessity, not a pleasure to him. The only shops he entered willingly were antique and furniture shops. He developed a great liking for poking round junk shops as he grew older, and he used to buy some beautiful pieces of furniture. To me they were nothing but a misery, as I was constantly nagged to be careful of them. 'Can't you keep your arse still? I don't want to see you kicking and spanning about!' I would be told. Father, who under normal conditions talked 'Norfolk', felt for some reason that expensive furniture-buying called for a more sophisticated accent, and he tried to match his to the quality of the merchandise. The grandest furniture shop in Norwich was Trevor Page, and it produced a strong reaction in Father. Mother said that 'there wasn't no need for him to start frimicating in a shop' but my sisters enjoyed it and if at any time they heard Father putting on his best English they said he was 'talking Trevor Page'.

In the normal course of events Mother and Father did not go out together for pleasure unless it was to buy furniture. Father had his 'rounds' and his pals at the markets, and Mother had the village social

86

life. Occasionally they would put on their black funeral suits and go off together to an important funeral, but Father only went if someone special was being buried. Once or twice they went to a wedding, but nothing more. Anything else was a family outing, such as going to the beach at Gorleston. Indeed Father never even went out to a pub in the evenings; he went at midday with his customers and cronies when he attended a market. Otherwise he did his drinking at home. Although he put back considerable quantities of whisky he still adopted a very prim attitude to social drinking, doubtless a left-over influence from his chapel upbringing, and he used to view other people's drinking habits with disapproval. He was fond of quoting a favourite verse to us as an awful warning.

> 'If all the world was bread and cheese,
> And all the sea was ink,
> There'd be no paupers in the land
> Because there'd be no drink.'

I was not very impressed with it, because I knew that Mother was sticking stamp paper on the whisky bottle to mark the level of the contents so that she could check the amount Father drank after she had gone to bed. Sometimes she resorted to hiding the bottle. Her favourite place was in the grandfather clock, but Father soon discovered it and simply emptied the bottle and put it back again for Mother to find. If, in later years, Father saw me hold up a bottle to the light to see how much it contained, he cried out in pain. 'For God's sake don't do that, girl,' he said. 'That's what I always see your mother do!'

Both my parents were very house-proud, and although Father and Mother invariably disagreed over everything they managed to enjoy their furniture-buying sprees, and continually replaced the sofa and easy chairs with new ones. Mother 'had a mind' for a three-piece suite in brown leather for the big room, and when she got it she made our lives hell worrying over it. If I scratched it she got very angry and nagged for hours. I soon learned that the best way to camouflage a new scratch was to spit on it and rub in a little dirt. That took the glaring raw newness out of it and if Mother noticed it she said, 'There now! That girl [meaning the maid] have scratched my chair again. She must have done that when the room was turned out. That wasn't done today,' and off she went to scold the unfortunate maid instead of me. When a new three-piece suite arrived, our old one was always passed on to Aunt Eliza. 'That'll do for Eliza,' Father said, and next day one of the mill lorries came and took the things to Lacton Mill House. Over the years Aunt Eliza received uncomplainingly our cast-off chairs and sofas of many makes and colours, letting the previous ones go to a second-hand shop. Father never expected her to have any opinion about what he dumped on her, and if she would have preferred to keep her old furniture, or rather Father's older pieces, she knew better than to say so.

Mother did all the household shopping either in the village or in Lacton. At any time of day Father was liable to burst into the house calling out, 'Do you want to go into Lacton? Well, look alive together and get your hats on.' Then Mother had to rush round collecting up her shopping basket and other odds and ends, and telling the maids what to do in her absence. If she were slow about it, Father got impatient and went out and sat in the car and sounded the horn to hurry her up. When finally she got into the car he drove to the town like a madman. The more annoyed he felt at the delay the faster he went. Mother seemed quite impervious to these tactics, but I was not, and always hoped fervently that she would do nothing to rile him before we had to go out in the car. The road to Lacton was a winding one, over the causeway, and we had to negotiate three narrow hump-backed bridges. 'Let the other buggers get out of the way!' Father said, as he positioned his big car in the middle of a blind bridge. If any other road-user got in Father's way and held up his progress he was furious. He considered it his right to pass everything on the road. 'I don't like to see anything in front of me,' he would say, and with his driving and the small amount of traffic on the move in those days, he was seldom behind another vehicle for long. When the local paper printed a report of a car accident Mother made a point of reading it aloud to us. 'There you are,' she commented, 'they were going too fast. If they hadn't been going too fast they would have been able to stop.' 'Don't talk so soft, don't,' Father replied. 'You mean the fools weren't going fast enough to get out of the way.'

Our dresses, and we had a lot of them, were made in Lacton by the dressmaker. She was Miss Lord, and her partner, who was the

junior partner, was Miss Barnard. Miss Lord wore a discreet, long black dress with a modesty vest and a velvet neck band, and her beautiful white hair was piled high on the top of her head in a big bun. She had a pin-cushion perpetually tied to her left wrist. I could not imagine her taking it off, even at bed time. Her house, or the part of it which we knew, consisted of a waiting room and a fitting room. They were divided by a magnificent bead curtain. It had long turquoise blue beads and a little round shiny brown ones, which in some places changed to green or red. I used to play with it and let it run through my fingers while Mother stood to be fitted in her pink celanese petticoat. Miss Lord adored Father, whom she had known for years. Her father, Oliver Lord, had owned the general stores in Lacton, and the family lived over the shop. When Father was a little boy he and his friends used to have great sport with that shop. In the evenings, after it was closed, they would kneel down in front of the shop and fold their hands in prayer. Reading from the printed sign over the shop front above their heads they chanted, 'O. Lord, Grocer and Draper, Sunlight Soap and Watson's Matchless Cleanser.' Father said they never had time to chant more than that before Oliver Lord got downstairs from his living quarters and rushed out of the shop in a fury. They had to run to escape.

Although the new fashion was for short hair, nearly all the ladies Mother knew still had long hair which they wore in a bun. Father made it clear that he liked long hair on a woman; in fact he forbade Mother to have hers cut. At the dressmakers we were able to look at all the fashion magazines while we waited for Mother. They showed pictures of very thin ladies with very smart dresses and the very latest short hairstyles, shingles, bobs and Eton crops. Skinny and Milly were thoroughly sick of their long hair. They had it tied back into big ribbon bows on the backs of their heads, and Skinny still had her beautiful, dark ringlet curls. Milly's hair was naturally straight as a poker but Mother refused to admit defeat and always insisted on trying to make it curl. It was not surprising that they wanted to have their hair cut, and they pestered Mother to allow them to do so. She flatly refused, but she had reckoned without Skinny, who always got her own way before long. One evening when Mother had left us whilst she went out to a meeting in the village, Skinny asked me if I would like to cut her hair. At that time I greatly fancied myself as a hairdresser and had cut the hair of all my dolls. I even clipped any of my toy animals which had fur long enough to make that possible, so I jumped at the chance to cut a real person's hair. Skinny stood in the middle of the play room and I climbed on to a chair and took the scissors which she handed to me. Then I cut and snipped until all her dark curls lay on the lino floor. Mother came home and stood aghast. Skinny said that I had wanted to cut her hair, but Mother was not deceived. 'You egged her on,' she said. But there was nothing to be done about it and next day Mother took both the girls to a hairdresser. Skinny had a bob and Milly, always one to go to extremes, had an Eton crop. It suited her. Whilst she was at the hairdressers Mother got her courage up and decided to have her own hair cut too. She knew Father had forbidden it, but that only stiffened her resolve. 'I aren't going to pay no regard to him,' she said. When they got home and confronted him Father surprised them by saying very little. He never said much when he could see that he was well and truly beaten. Perhaps he really liked the short hair, after all, but if so he would have known better than to have admitted it to

Mother. She would have viewed a willingness to change his mind as a sign of weakness, a crack in his armour. Mother was so carried away by the success of the hair cuts that she 'got beyond herself'. She fell in love with a new dress material called sponge cloth. It was all the rage. She had Miss Lord make up dresses in it for herself and the girls. This time Father was outraged. 'I hate that old stuff,' he told her. 'That's only an old bit of towelling rag.' Mother's dress soon disappeared, and nothing more was said.

Father used to leave us at the dressmaker's house while he went to visit Lacton Mill and look in at Aunt Eliza's office. Sometimes, when he arrived to pick us up again, anxious to get home to his dinner, Miss Barnard still had Mother in the fitting room, covered in cloth and pins. Miss Lord was a person of unruffled dignity. Doubtless she could well remember Father as a naughty little boy, as she was a good deal older than my parents. 'You go on fitting,' she instructed her junior partner. 'I'll go and tell him that we won't be long.' Out she sailed, leaving all of us, including Mother, gasping in admiration. Through the waiting room window I could see her go up to the car and engage Father in animated conversation. He opened the car window wide and they talked through it; he did not consider it necessary to get out. Obviously they enjoyed whatever passed between them. He laughed and she laughed. After a few minutes Miss Lord returned to the house with her cheeks glowing pink and her pretty blue eyes dancing. When we got out to the car Father was in high good humour. Usually he complained bitterly if he was not out of the town by twelve-thirty when the hooter at 'the works' sounded, and the roads were packed with frantic cyclists going home to their dinners. He was astonished that they showed no respect for his big car, and refused to give way to him, but even that did not put him out after Miss Lord had made him laugh.

Things like shoes and coats which Mother did not buy in Lacton came from Norwich. Father went to all the local markets in the course of his business, and every Saturday was Norwich market. When Mother wanted to shop there we all went with him. He needed to leave the house by twelve noon, so we were given an early lunch and dashed out in great disorder. Mother was never ready, and we went through the car hooter routine every time. The later we started the more we saw on the road, that is to say, the more we overtook because all the traffic was going the same way as we approached the city. Those were the days when cattle were driven on the hoof to the market on Norwich Hill, right in the centre of the city. It was almost impossible to get past the herds of bullocks, or sometimes flocks of sheep, and if you got past one lot you were very soon stuck behind the next. The drovers, nearing Norwich, had probably been walking half the night as well as all that morning and were in no mood to be co-operative with motor cars. Father tooted his horn. He was reluctant to push too close to the cattle in case they damaged his car, so he had to content himself with winding down the window and shouting and swearing at the men. Sometimes they shouted back. There was not much they could do to get a car through such a throng of animals even if they had not already decided to let the old fool of a driver go to hell.

When we got to Norwich Father insisted on parking his car in the Boar's Head yard. The entrance, between the brick walls of two buildings, allowed the Daimler to pass with about two inches spare space on either side. Father took this as a challenge and would never have considered parking anywhere else. He negotiated the entrance to the yard with a triumphant flourish that left his passengers cowering. As soon as the car came to rest he would leap out. 'Jarrolds at four o'clock,' he called to Mother, over his shoulder, as he rushed for the Corn Hall where his customers were waiting. Then Mother gathered herself together and marched us off to do the shopping. The bills must have been enormous. She usually bought a pair of shoes for each of us children, and sometimes two pairs for herself as well. She never paid cash nor carried the parcels away with her; she had them sent to the Boar's Head, and the shops' accounts came in later by post. Next Mother took us to Greens to buy coats and hats. School uniform came from Greens, on the Walk. There, black pudding-basin hats were crammed on to my head by conscientious shop assistants. My ears were left sticking out under the brim. Comfort was not considered. Mother bought clothes for herself at Greens too, in the Ladies Department. She selected suitable garments and retired with them into the ladies' fitting room. It had red-and-blue stained glass in an art nouveau pattern in the top half of the door which separated it from the rest of the shop. I was kindly directed to ride the large faded rocking-horse, provided by a thoughtful management to keep impatient children occupied. It was a feeble creature in comparison with Dobbin, our own beautiful rocking-horse at home. Dobbin had started life a dappled grey, and now he was old and had not much tail left, but he was still my fiery steed with scarlet nostrils, and much better than the horse at Greens, which, to my scorn, was set on wooden runners, securely fixed to the floor. Milly could rock our horse so high and so hard that she made him advance right across the summer house floor. He was a grand beast.

The parcels from Greens, like those from the shoe shop, were all sent to the Boar's Head where the car was parked. Occasionally, when the school shopping was finished, Mother let us children go off by ourselves. We had strict instructions to get to Jarrolds in time to meet Father for tea. Milly and I used to make straight for our favourite cockle stall on the market. Cockles were a half-penny a saucer. One grabbed the saucer and, squeezing the cockles flat into one's fingers, tipped it up to let the excess water run off onto the cobble stones of the market place. We had to practise hard to do this with a real old-timer's nonchalance, but we liked to think we achieved it. It never occurred to us that the other patrons of the stall, mostly country men out for the day, might find the presence of two children amusing, and we tackled it in deadly earnest. If anyone laughed we did not notice. There were vinegar and salt and pepper to go with the cockles, and the stall sold mussels, whelks, winkles and all manner of other shellfish too. We piled up the empty saucers in front of us until we had either eaten our fill or run out of money. I had to stop and count my saucers every now and then to make sure I had not overspent. When we had finished the stall-holder ran a dirty finger over the pile and announced the total score. My record was fourteen saucers. After that we went off to tea.

Jarrolds at four o'clock, he had said, and sure enough Father was always there at the appointed time. If anyone was late it was Milly and me. Tea began with bread and butter or toast, and Father always offered cake. Mother asked him to order what she called 'cut cake', a rather dull currant loaf. Father laughed and asked Milly if she would like cream cakes, which she adored. When the trolley came to our table she chose a cake bulging with cream, a cream horn or an éclair. Father said, 'Goodbye, Milly, goodbye!' and laughed, delighted, but Mother frowned and said that cream cakes were sickly old things. After the cakes I waited expectantly, wondering if Father could possibly forget what came next. He never did, and solemnly asked if I would like an ice cream. I had a round pink one in a metal dish on a long stem, so tall that I had to sit up very straight to be able to reach into it with my spoon. A triangular wafer was stuck in the top of the pink mound, and the metal dish was cloudy with the cold. It was a perfect tea. At that time Jarrolds was in its heyday. Under the glass-domed skylight in the centre of the restaurant was a circular pen with a wooden rail around it. In this the orchestra played, surrounded by huge potted palms. It was not meant to be cheerful, just elegant, and the musicians scraped away at their instruments. Sometimes people danced on the uncarpeted area of floor outside the orchestra pen, but we did not often see dancing on just an ordinary Saturday. Although it was the era of the tea dance, the management found it could do better serving the maximum number of teas when the farmers came in on a Saturday, than by leaving space for dancing, and usually the tables were allowed to encroach on to the dance floor.

After tea we set off for the Boar's Head. In my memories it was always a winter afternoon and we were wearing warm coats. Father led me through the dark wet streets, with the pavements shining in the shop lights. A lighted shopping street on a dark winter afternoon has held a special magic for me ever since my childhood. Back at the Boar's Head our parcels had been piled into Father's car in readiness for us. 'My heart and eyes!' he said, surveying the mountain of boxes. 'I reckon you must have bought the Dickens over the baulk today!' Mother had to count the parcels and fuss round before we could start for home. Once a parcel was missing. Shoes, Mother said, so Father telephoned the shoe shop from some mysterious place inside the Boar's Head. We all waited, sitting in the car, whilst a boy on a bicycle brought the missing box from the shop. Father was not best pleased to be kept waiting, but in spite of that, because it was dark, he managed to drive home at quite a moderate pace.

Father liked to take Jack with him when he attended Norwich market. At the time when Mother had worked in the mill office, Jack had been an apprentice and she had taught him to do the accounts. Now he still worked for Father and went to market with him to write down the orders in his pocket book. Norwich market was important because it was a market especially for the sale of grain, held in the big Corn Hall. Father had a stand there with his name on it. It was a small, high wooden desk at which Jack had to remain to do business whilst Father roamed round the hall meeting friends and customers and taking the latter out for drinks. The pubs in Norwich kept open all day on Saturdays for that purpose, he assured us. In the car coming home from our shopping expeditions in Norwich we played 'I spy' with Jack. We could talk and joke with him then, but as soon as we got home he had to be left quiet until he had copied the orders out of his pocket book ready for Monday morning. That done, Mother, who invariably was in the kitchen getting supper ready, said, 'Ask Jack to come and wash his hands and cut the bread and butter.' Mother found Jack's visits useful for more than cutting bread and butter; she held him up as an example to us of how we ought to behave. When she said, 'Jack was never allowed to do that when he was a little boy, were you, Jack?' he had to say no, he was not, but he said it with a sheepish grin so that it did not always ring true, and we knew that secretly he was on our side. After supper Jack used to play with us. More often than not we played draughts. This was one of the few games Father was ever willing to play himself. I never liked it because my opponents were always much too crafty for me; in fact I did not enjoy that sort of game at all. Father and Jack won at draughts and Milly won at snap and pelmanism. I never won, unless, being the youngest, I was allowed to do so on purpose, and that was worse than being beaten in fair fight. I do not think that Skinny ever won, either, except at Happy Families, but she did not seem to care in the least.

I looked forward to those Saturday evenings when Jack came. A thing at which he really excelled was peeling an apple so that the skin came off in one long unbroken coil. This was invaluable at Hallowe'en when you had to peel an apple and throw the long worm of skin over your shoulder. After it fell to the floor you decided which letter of the alphabet the tangled shape resembled and that was the initial letter of your future wife's or husband's Christian name. It led to some surprising speculation. Hallowe'en, when Jack was with us, was always fun. One year Skinny and I went out in the dark to pull up cabbages. The shape of the cabbage predicted the build of a future husband, tall or short, lean or tubby, and Skinny and I were keen to know what fate

held in store for us. It was not a very dark night, but we had difficulty in finding the cabbages we wanted. Of course it was supposed to be too dark to see what you got, but that did not influence us and we pulled up a lot of cabbages before we felt we could be certain of the tall thin husbands we required. I wanted one just like Jack. When Father saw what we had done to his vegetable garden he was furious. 'That had been different,' he said, 'if you hadn't known no better.'

There was one Saturday in the year when we were never allowed to go to Norwich, and that was the weekend of the Tombland Fair. Father and Jack had to go so as not to miss any orders, but they came home early. On Tombland Fair Saturday the Corn Hall was taken over by drunks who threw ink pots at one another, Father said. They had been known to break up the wooden stands and start fights. We heard shocking stories about it. I always wanted to see for myself what went on, but I was told that was out of the question. It was the same at Lacton May Fair. This was an old horse fair, and when we were children the local point-to-point races were held on the same day. We went to the races with Mother, but Father disapproved of it. He feared that we might get into the habit of betting and go to the bad. 'I don't hold with no gambling,' he said. Instead, when he had finished work he took us to the fair and we had rides on the steam horses, and Jack came on the Cake-walk with us. There was a lot of fun and laughter, but we were always hurried home from the fair before the late evening when things were expected to get rough. Father was good at hitting coconuts, and he never failed to get one for us from the coconut shy. I could not throw the little wooden ball hard enough to dislodge a coconut, even though, being so small, I was allowed to throw from inside the front barrier. The owners of the stalls piled up sawdust all round each coconut to keep them from falling too easily, and you had to be a crack shot, like Father, to knock one down. The fair rock which Father bought for us was splendid. We could have a small pink stick with a piece of paper wrapped round one end, and hold it while we sucked, or we could choose a bag of multi-coloured broken pieces of rock to take home. The brown pieces with a swirling marbled pattern running through them were the best. They tasted of cloves.

Although Mother maintained that Jack's behaviour had usually been perfect she was forced to admit that just once when he had been a little boy he had done a shocking thing. It must have been the worst thing he ever did: he saw Father Christmas. He pretended to go to sleep on Christmas Eve, but secretly he kept watch until Father Christmas came into the bedroom, and Jack actually saw him. I never tired of hearing this terrible story, which ended with the sad fact that Father Christmas never came to Jack again. At that time I believed in Father Christmas without any reservation, and Jack's story merely confirmed my faith. On Christmas Eve, encouraged by Father, I left out a bottle of whisky and a glass on the wireless room table for Father Christmas, before I went up to bed and hung up my stocking. (We had to leave the whisky and the glass on a tray, otherwise Mother would have complained that it marked the table.) Anxiously I asked Father if he thought that Father Christmas would find the whisky and Father said he was certain that he would. When I was in bed I shut my eyes tightly and never opened them again until morning because I did not want to make Jack's mistake. In the morning I rushed downstairs to see if Father Christmas had found the whisky and sure enough, there was the used glass beside the bottle, proof positive that he had been in the house, if my stocking bulging with presents were not proof enough. This procedure repeated itself happily enough for several years until one day in early December I was playing in the drawing room, where I had no business to be, and found a stack of parcels underneath the sofa frill. Hidden there I saw games, books and dolls. I dare not say a word about finding them, but, horror of horrors, on Christmas Day the very same parcels appeared in our Christmas stockings, and all my illusions were shattered. I managed to survive the shock without breathing a word about my discovery to anyone, and continued politely but hollowly to go through the motions of believing in Father Christmas so that he would, in some form at least, continue to operate. I had Jack to thank for this foresight. I would have never have known the importance of keeping my own counsel but for the awesome story of his untimely disaster.

IX

It was 1926, and the time of the General Strike. Mother and I looked out of her bedroom window and saw Father across the yard. He was standing on the office step, which was half of an old mill wheel, talking to a little knot of men gathered in front of him. I asked Mother what was happening and she said that it was the General Strike, and Father was telling his men that if any of them went on strike he would never have them to work for him again. When he stopped speaking they all trooped back to work, which was not surprising since almost all of them were living in Father's houses. In any case, although Father was generally known to be a hard businessman, he was not thought unfair and most of those who came to work for him stayed with him for the rest of their lives.

By the standards of those days the mill was considered a sizeable business. Father was very go-ahead about machinery and much preferred motors to horses. He said no one had to get up before breakfast to feed the buggers like they did horses, and he had enough of that as a boy. I can remember him keeping only one horse-drawn wagon, and he got rid of that after a while. Sometimes I went for a ride with Father in his car if he were going on a short round and on one of these occasions we overtook his wagon. The driver was trying to hurry the two huge carthorses into a trot, presumably to get home to his tea on time, and their great plumed feet were raising a cloud of dust. Father stopped him and swore at him. The horses were beautiful, valuable beasts and it made Father wild to see them misused. 'Do you do that again and you'll get the sack,' he shouted at the man, 'trying to ruin my bloody horses!' Then he got back into the car and drove on as fast as possible to relieve his feelings.

Although Father loved motors he was not above a few economies at the expense of other road users, and until driving mirrors were made compulsory on all lorries, Father refused to have them fitted to his. One day Mother's favourite doctor, Dr Rodwell, was following one of Father's lorries down a narrow and dusty road, and although he sounded his horn repeatedly he failed to attract the lorry driver's attention. He wanted to get past, and he was being smothered in dust.

Eventually the road widened out and Dr Rodwell passed the lorry, but by that time he was so cross that he stopped Father's driver and complained. He asked the man to tell his employer that his lorries were a menace on the road and that he ought to have mirrors fitted to all of them. A few weeks later Dr Rodwell got behind the same lorry on the same stretch of road and again he could not pass it. Once more he was choked with dust and as soon as he could do so he stopped the driver again. 'Well, my man,' he said, 'did you give your employer my message?' 'Yes,' said the lorry driver. 'Well, what did he say?' asked Dr Rodwell. 'He said you can tell Dr Rodwell to go to buggery!' the man replied. This incident gave Father great pleasure. Doctors failed to impress him. He thought they were a necessary evil, and luckily he did not need one very often. In contrast Mother respected doctors. In fact she made such a fuss when the doctor came that it was remarkable that we children did not develop a fear of doctors. She simpered and fluttered round Dr Rodwell, but Father's attitude was more robust altogether.

In the early days Father kept an enormous steam lorry as well as the horses. I was really frightened of it because it was very black and made such a terrible noise. It had a big rounded front with high seat for the driver, and he was always very black too. All the drivers who worked at the mill had to clean their own lorries and sometimes Father would send me to the lorry shed to tell a certain man that he wanted to see him before he 'left off'. If Father wanted the steam lorry driver I rushed out of the shed again as soon as I had given the message. Really the steam lorry was very beautiful with its red and gold squiggles painted between thin gold lines which formed a border decoration all round it, but I could never appreciate it at the time. Later Father only kept more modern lorries, and each year he got bigger and better ones. Only one little old-fashioned lorry remained until the last, and that was driven by our friend Goggles. Poor old Goggles loved his little lorry, and Father did not have the heart to get rid of it while the old man could still drive, so the small lorry stood proudly beside the grand modern ones in the lorry shed and proved very handy for small loads and short journeys.

Most of Father's men had worked for him since he was a young man, and some, like Goggles, had worked for Grand-dad. Father had his favourites, and they used to come and tell him their troubles and get what help and advice he could give them. He knew their wives and families and all their domestic problems, and Mother knew them all too. Often the wives confided in Mother and the husbands in Father. One of Father's best-loved employees was Jimmy. He was quiet-spoken, unsmiling, reliable sort of man, and one of Father's best lorry drivers. Unfortunately he was married to a very lively, sexy woman who soon took on the duties of village tart, so perhaps Jimmy had not got much to smile about. She set her cap at carrot-haired Fiske who looked after our garden. He cleaned the cars, and he had to drive Mother about if Father did not wish to do so himself. The tarty lady was so bold as to come into the mill-yard and talk to Fiske in the garage whilst he was polishing the car. They got away with it until one day when Father came home unexpectedly and went into the garage and caught them, and gave Fiske the sack on the spot. Mrs Fiske, whom Mother considered a nice little woman, came to plead with Mother to persuade Father to change his mind, but there was nothing Mother could do. Father said that if he did not make an example of Fiske, then all his men might think they could have their fancy women on the place, and then where would he be? They would not get much work done like that, he said. Fiske and his family had to get out of Father's cottage and eventually left the district.

Soon after they left, it became apparent that Mrs Jimmy was 'in the family way', and she gave birth to a red-headed son, just like Fiske. It was not unknown for something like that to happen in the village, and no one took much notice. Jimmy had to accept the baby into his family, but he must have felt sore about it, as there was no getting away from the flaming red hair. Anyway, after that matters went from bad to worse between him and his wife. We heard reports that Mrs Jimmy was always 'out after the men' every night and that she was bringing her eldest daughter up to do the same. It was said in the village that his wife came down to breakfast in the middle of the morning, after Jimmy had gone to work, with the last night's make-up still on her unwashed face. Her neighbours could understand and perhaps forgive her being a tart but they could not get over her dirty face. That really shocked them. Jimmy used to tell Father his side of the story, and get what sympathy he could. Then the situation reached a climax. Mrs Jimmy wrote a note to Mother asking her to get Father to speak to Jimmy, and tell him to mend his ways. She wrote that Jimmy had come out in boils because he had refused to give her his 'married love' as was her due. Mother was incapable of thinking of a suitable answer, so she and Father decided to ignore the note and the trouble blew over into an armed truce.

People like Jimmy could not expect to get a divorce or separation in those times. It was unheard of. They had no money and nowhere to go to escape, and there was no question of legal aid. A divorce would have shocked the village. Any 'goings on' were better done in wedlock than out of it, so while they could not solve their domestic troubles they just had to soldier on and make the best of a bad job. At least by doing so Jimmy kept the respect and friendship of his neighbours.

Another time when Father was asked to speak to an erring husband he did so with disastrous results. One day, walking through Lacton, he was stopped by Mrs W. She told Father that her husband, who was one of his employees, was getting drunk every Saturday night and coming home, breaking up the furniture and frightening the children. Father felt sorry for her, so when she asked him to use his influence to persuade her husband to turn over a new leaf, he agreed to try. Father talked to the man, and then thought no more about it until a few months later he saw the wife in the town again and crossed the road to speak to her. He asked if her husband's behaviour had improved. 'Oh, Sir!' she said, 'I wish you hadn't never said nothing to him. He joined the Salvation Army after what you said, and he give up the drink and got saved. Now he plays in the brass band and he practise at home in the front room of an evening. The noise he make is terrible, that's worse than what that was when he was drunk.'

Although the amorous Fiske was employed to look after the car, and later two cars, driving a smaller one which was kept for Mother's use and for taking my sisters to school, he was never allowed to drive Father's Daimler. Usually Father liked to drive himself but there were special occasions when he felt that the journey was going to be arduous, and then he would call upon the services of Mr Catchpole. When Father needed him to drive the car Mr Catchpole had to be warned in good time so that he could go home and get washed and changed. He was always dirty, especially his hands, as befitted an engineer. He was

102

no talker, a dour but very superior man, and Father had taken him on when the expansion of the business and installation of modern machinery had made more work than Bob could manage. Mr Catchpole was considered a cut above Bob in many ways, and only Father himself ever called him Billy. Driving through Norwich one busy afternoon, with Father beside him, Mr Catchpole was seen to smile. Father was directing him and said, 'Down King Street, Billy, and mind the kids!' At that time King Street was a very poor housing area, swarming with children playing in the roadway. Father did not like having to be careful when he was driving himself, but he rather enjoyed telling Mr Catchpole how to do it. Because Father liked to sit in front when Mr Catchpole was driving, Mother had to get into the back of the car. If they were going a long way and the weather was cold, Father told Mother to 'find up' the car rug. It was an otter-skin rug, and he liked to see it put across Mother's knees in the car. He was proud of that rug because all the otters had been killed on his own stretch of river. Otters were not protected then, and they ate the fish and eels, so Father looked upon them as his natural enemies. Each skin, and there was a row of them, was spread out in a crucified attitude and stitched on to a navy-blue cloth backing. There were ghastly blind holes where the otters' eyes would have been, and all the whiskers had been left on the faces so that the rug was very prickly. I do not know where Father got the rug made up, but anyway, he was delighted with it.

Mr Catchpole may have been a good engineer but no one felt the same affection for him as they did for Bob. Dear Bob! He could find a way to mend anything and he had a total scorn for 'new-fangled' methods and mass-produced machines. 'They aren't nothing only tin and string,' he said sadly, shaking his head. 'Tin and string.' When Father needed Bob he could usually find him either in the dark, cold blacksmith's shop, with its smell of iron filings and grease, or else in the carpenter's shop, knee-deep in fragrant wood shavings. There, where the cobwebs hung like lace curtains at the windows, Bob would be standing, working at the long bench. 'Bob,' Father asked, 'have you got that there what's-er-name?' and Bob would put down what he was doing, straighten up and smile with his twinkly blue eyes. 'Why, what what's-er-name is that?' he enquired, deadly serious. Father never lost patience with Bob. 'Why, you know,' he told him, 'one of them

what's-er-names what come from old John's last summer.' Sure enough, Bob knew what Father meant. 'Oh ah!' he said, and shuffled off through the wood shavings to produce the very thing from some special drawer or dark forgotten corner. 'You never want to throw nothing away, because that'll always come in,' Bob advised us. 'Everything come in once in seven years.'

The very old mill carpenter was Bob's best friend. They had been working together all their lives, and Mother said that when those two put their heads together there was nothing they could not contrive. Father was incapable of leaving anyone alone to get on with a job. He felt compelled, having told a man what was wanted, not only to go at frequent intervals to see if the task was being carried out, but also to tell the worker exactly how to do it. He went on like that all the time, even when dealing with his most experienced craftsmen, and it was amazing how well they managed to put up with this dreadful habit. Most of them used to turn unaccountably deaf when Father approached, but in the end one of the worms turned. Bob's old carpenter friend, who boasted a walrus moustache and really did carry his tools in a triangular sacking bag, like the Carpenter in 'Alice', had been sent to repair a bedroom window. He was at the top of the ladder and getting on nicely, when Father came into the garden and started telling him a better way to do the job. The old man climbed stiffly down the ladder. When he reached the ground he flung his tools down at Father's feet and shouted, 'Yap, yap, yap! Do your bloody work yourself!' and marched off home. Father was dumb-founded. Then he was furious, not only because the old carpenter had answered back, but also because all of us inside the house had heard what had been said. Mother kept reminding him of it; she just could not leave it alone. 'You'll have to go and apologise to him,' she told Father. 'Bob won't stop with you if that old boy goes.' Father declared that nothing would induce him to ask the carpenter to return. This state of affairs went on for a day or two. I do not know who picked up the carpenter's tools from the garden but it is certain that Father did not do so. Then Bob must have threatened to leave, just as Mother had guessed he would, because mysteriously the carpenter came back to work the next week and Father refused to discuss what had happened. After that we called the old carpenter 'Yap-yap'. All the employees called him that too, on the quiet, so that Father was never allowed to forget the incident, even though he chose to ignore it. We children thought Yap-yap was a hero and loved him for getting the better of Father.

At that time Father dealt with the Lacton blacksmith. He was what would now be called an agricultural engineer. He supplied all the pipes and odds and ends which Father could not get made up in his own blacksmith's shop and which were not part of the specialised milling machinery. The Lacton blacksmith had not got the right feeling of respect for Father and would not go out of his way to be obliging. He did not always deliver on time. Occasionally this attitude brought Father's temper, always quick to rise, to boiling point. Then he got into his car and started off with a crashing and grinding of gears. 'I'll go after that bugger, go to hell if I won't,' he said, and he turned the big Daimler into the entrance to the blacksmith's yard. It was a very narrow passage and no one could squeeze past the big car, even on foot, if they were carrying a load, so Father effectively brought business to a standstill. Then he got out, inching himself out of the car door, and looked round for Mr Rushmer. By that time the blacksmith was incensed at the blockage Father had caused on the premises, and he came out of his office ready to give as good as he got. They were always quarrelling with one another and continued the feud all their lives. In their retirement years a good scrap used to cheer them up. When Father was in his sixties they met one day in the town just after Father had recovered from the serious illness which had beset him at that time. Mr Rushmer told Father that it was unwise to put too much faith in his recovery. After all, Grand-dad had died at the age of sixty-four, he reminded him. Father could not forgive this remark. 'What do you think that bugger said?' he asked me in amazement. As usual Father was determined to retaliate, and bided his time until one day when Mr Rushmer was complaining about the cost of living. 'No one can't afford to live these days,' the blacksmith said. Then Father drew himself up with great dignity. 'Well, Mr Rushmer,' he replied, 'I reckon you'll have to live because, with the death duties as they are, that's one thing certain, you can't afford to die. Good day,' and he marched off. Father always said 'good day'. He told me it saved him having to remember whether it was morning or afternoon, and he did not want any clever bugger telling him he had made a mistake.

There was no room in Father's life for hobbies; he was too occupied with his business. He enjoyed trying to get the better of anyone, and in this he usually succeeded. After he had dealt with the office and the mill, been out on his rounds and to the markets and had a walk round looking for rats in the evenings, there was not much spare time. The little time he had to himself he used to spend reading. He took two local papers as well as a London daily and *The Miller*. Father was very interested in the milling competitions promoted by or advertised in *The Miller* and he liked to enter his products whenever he could. He had a whole drawer full of medals which he had won for his flour: gold and silver ones, and a few bronze, and he had a large silver cup too. Naturally he was very proud of his cup and when he received it all his employees were invited to drink out of it to celebrate the success. Father collected a lot of certificates too, and the early ones were framed and hung up in the office, until he got so many that he ran out of wall space.

The office was a long narrow room smelling of meal and flour. There were desks all along one side, under the windows, high brown desks at which the clerks stood, or sat on stools, writing in the massive ledgers and 'day books' which were all kept by hand in beautiful copperplate writing. The cupboards which lined the back of the office, where it was rather dark, were full of old ledgers and papers. Some of the bills and receipts were kept on long bill-hooks and hung up in bunches, gathering dust, the bottom papers already brown and curling at the edges. Father did not do the accounts himself, nor any of the writing if he could help it. His handwriting was shocking, almost unreadable, and his spelling was even worse. Mother was inclined to be superior about this because she was good at spelling as well as having been trained in accountancy. Father just refused to bother about spelling. If anyone dared to criticise or tell him he had misspelt a word in one of his rare written notes, he would say, 'Did you know what I meant by that word?' When the unfortunate critic had to admit, feeling put in the wrong already by Father's haughty manner, that he did, Father told him, 'All right, that served the purpose then, didn't it?' I much admired him for putting people down in this masterly fashion and wished I dared to do the same, for I had inherited his blind spot for spelling.

The office was divided into two sections. In the first part the junior clerks worked at the day-to-day routine, and people came to the counter to bring loading invoices or pay bills. The inner office was the newest part which Father had added when the business grew bigger, and was special, just for Father and his head clerk, Mr Suggett. Father liked to sit there and talk to people, and it was there that he cut loaves of bread in halves to examine them and see if the baker had done justice to the flour. Mr Suggett stood all day at his desk in the new office, checking other people's mistakes and getting ready for the annual audit.

Before Mr Suggett came Mother had done the auditing herself, and she was rather proud of it. The junior clerk used to bring the big ledgers across from the office to the house, one or two at a time, as they could be spared, and Mother spread them out on the dining table and 'did the books'. If any of the clerks' writing or figures were unclear she told Father about it. She said things had never been like that when she was in the office. Once Mr Suggett was installed Father gave the job of auditing to him. Mother never forgave Father for that. 'He took the books away from me,' Mother said. 'He was afraid I should know too much.'

Mr Suggett was a tiny, sallow-faced little man, with a hooked nose like Mr Punch. Standing in his office, he always wore his hat. We could see him through the window. He sucked his empty pipe and said nothing. He had a large fleshy wife and five children, and they lived in Father's most coveted house at the end of the row in the lane. His wife said Mr Suggett never spoke. She said he had got out of the habit of speaking before he came to work for Father. He had been sworn to secrecy in a Yarmouth office, she said, and had 'never opened his face since'. Mrs Suggett was a foreigner. She was a native of Great Yarmouth and spoke with a different accent from the rest of the village people. Anyone coming from more than fifteen miles distant was considered a foreigner until they had lived half a lifetime in the village. Mrs Suggett was accepted, if with reservation, because her husband, like Bob, had become a cornerstone of the business and no one could imagine Father managing without him.

As well as winning so many medals and awards for milling, Father also had his invention. Because our house was attached to the mill the noise of the night shift rattled and hummed through our bedrooms; it disturbed Mother, although the rest of the household hardly noticed it. When a new machine was installed to clean the wheat, Mother found it so noisy that she got no sleep at all and begged Father to do something about it. Bob and Father undertook to work out some improvements and eventually they invented a completely new wheat-cleaning machine which operated quietly. Then someone thought of getting a patent for it. Bob and Father were delighted, but as far as I know the machine was never taken up to be manufactured and the nine days' wonder fizzled out to become nothing more than a triumphant memory. They never made any money out of it.

Father used to take me into the mill quite often when I was a child. He taught me not to be afraid to climb the steep ladder stairs. My short legs could only just reach from step to step and I could look down three floors between the treads. The mill never seemed to be too noisy for me, just pleasantly throbbing and grinding. Father told me to avoid going up to one of the machines when a miller was working at it, so that the man could not see me coming. I must not startle the operator but approach from his front and speak in a normal voice. There was no need to shout because the millers were so used to the noise that they could hear you if you spoke quietly. All the millers seemed to be quiet men. They wore striped flannel collarless shirts and grey trousers, or navy bib-and-brace overalls, and they were always covered in dust. I do not think that special mill overalls had been thought of then, and no one considered that flour dust might do the workmen any harm. It covered them: their caps, which they kept on all the time, their clothes and their boots, even their eyebrows, were white with dust.

Sometimes Father took us into the mill to be weighed. One side of the weighing machine was a tall wooden cage, big enough to hold a full sack, and the weights were lifted on and off a tray on the other side by hand. I had to stand in the cage to be weighed while Father piled the weights on to the tray. The floor of the little weighing cage was a beautiful golden colour, the wood polished by the sliding on and off of a thousand heavy flour sacks. It smelt of meal and dust. We children were not supposed to go into the mill or the mill yard unless sent there to find Father, or on some other errand. Then we had to look out for the chains which hung into the yard from the loading bays three storeys up. Lorries stood under these and sacks of flour were winched down by the chains out of a trap door and placed on them for loading. A man worked on the back of the lorry directing the winchman above him and moving the sacks around to make a neat load. At other times the process was reversed and sacks of wheat were raised from the lorries by the chains and pulled up through the trapdoors to the top of the mill. The chain came rattling down again with some force after each sack had been lifted, and one had to keep out of the way to make sure of not being hit by it. Father said that when he was a boy he used to climb out of the trapdoor at Lacton Mill and his brothers winched him down clinging to the end of the chain. They took it in turns to get a ride. It was, of course, absolutely forbidden by Grand-dad but that did not stop them. Mother's brothers did it too. It was not difficult to imagine them all as children running round the mill and playing in the yard, living in that same Mill House all those years before us. I could understand why Father had wanted a son so that both mills could go on in the family for another generation.

X

Education was yet another subject of disagreement between my parents. Father openly derided it. He had hated going to school himself and deeply pitied anyone who had to be educated. When I cried because I did not want to go to school I had all his sympathy, but I got none from Mother. Father's early memories of school showed he had good reason to loathe it; they were grim. At first he was sent to a little dame school in Lacton along with the ill-fated butcher, Harry Taylor, and his brother George. In an old photograph of the three of them in a school group they are wearing sailor suits and enormous boots which dangled like weights from the ends of their stick-like legs as they huddled on the bench. Father looked very small, skinny and frightened. The children were taught by the schoolmaster and his wife, helped by their teenage son. Father said the wife was the worst. He told us that he recollected that the old bitch frightened him so much that one day he vomited into her lap. That was his moment of triumph. She was wearing a black satin apron embroidered with jet beads at the time. Another day he was shut in a dark cupboard as a punishment. He managed, in utter panic, to force his way out of a second door which led into a bedroom. He crept sobbing down the stairs and escaped, sneaking out of the house to run home and tell Grand-dad. The old man immediately came to Father's defence. He had a splendid row with the schoolmaster, and Father was removed and sent to Lacton Grammar School. There Father began to excel at art, which he loved. He painted a beautiful butterfly, only to have the teacher come and put a thick black line right across the whole picture. Father was devastated and retired to cry in the lavatory. From that day onwards he was at war with school.

Mother, in contrast, had an unholy passion for education. As a girl she had set her heart on becoming a schoolteacher but the family was in very poor circumstances, even before her father's early death. As she was the second eldest of nine children her education had to be ended abruptly to allow her to go out to work at the earliest possible age. Even during her short years at school she was subjected to repeated set-backs. Every time Grandmother had a new baby Mother had to miss school and stay at home to look after the house. She was determined to get her own back on fate by forcing as much education into her daughters as she possibly could. The only thing which hindered her was her complete inability to co-operate with anyone, least of all a school. Rules, in her opinion, were not made for her family. They were for those who were fools enough to comply with them and who had no minds of their own. Mother, to show her contempt, flouted the school rules at every turn. If the school asked for long-sleeved white dresses she sent us in short-sleeved cream ones and very often, to make matters worse, the dresses had embroidery on them too. If we were supposed to wear sleeveless black dancing dresses Mother bought long-sleeved ones because, she said, we should get our deaths of cold if she did otherwise. She put us through purgatory.

To begin their education my two sisters were sent to a genteel little school in Lacton. It was run by two respectable maiden ladies who were sisters, and they did all the teaching themselves. There, at a tender age, the girls learned all about God. They did not get a chance to learn it from Mother as, although she attended church every Sunday and was a respected member of the Mothers' Union, she did not hold with bringing religion into the house. Skinny was so struck by the story of Jesus that she really took it to heart. One day Mother found the two girls sitting side by side on the doorstep. Skinny was crying her eyes out and sobbing, 'Poor Jesus! Poor Jesus!' over and over again, while Milly stolidly repeated, 'Silly old Jesus! Silly old Jesus!' which, needless to say, made Skinny cry the harder. That quite unnecessary scene, Mother said, proved what a mistake it was to upset little children with a lot of old religion. It just showed that she knew best about that as she did about everything else.

Predictably Skinny went on to make her own unforgettable contribution to the richness of life in the infants class. When she stayed to school dinner for the first time the teacher said grace. 'That's not the same grace as my father says,' Skinny told her. The teacher showed kindly interest. 'Then you can tell us what your Father's grace is, dear,' she encouraged her angelic little pupil, and there, before the assembled school, Skinny recited,
'From rocks and sands and barren lands,
Good Lord deliver me!
And from great guns and women's tongues
Oh, good God, set me free!'

111

The schoolteacher's sense of humour could not rise to the occasion and she complained to Mother about it, but Mother was not at all abashed. She took it in her stride and declared that Skinny had not done any harm, in fact she might have done the old maids a lot of good.

When they were too old for the school in Lacton my sisters were sent to the Anglo-Catholic convent which was situated conveniently near our home, so that they could attend daily. 'Duzzy old nuns, sticking a lot of religion into the kids,' Father said ominously. Here again it was Skinny who got into trouble. She insisted on saying a long and complicated grace before every meal. She had learned it from the nuns at school where she soon developed into an ardent Christian and crossed herself ostentatiously at every opportunity. Father's own version of grace was the only one he was willing to hear in his house and he raised hell. He said he thought Skinny might go and wall herself up in some bloody convent. 'She's not right,' he said. 'I'll get her certified!' This was the usual remedy he threatened for any of Skinny's more lunatic pieces of behaviour, and Mother was terrified. 'He's quite capable of signing anything to get her put away,' she told us fearfully. In this she showed how implicitly she believed in Father's ability to get his own way in the face of any odds. Of course Father never expected any opposition; indeed waywardness in any of his daughters always astounded him. When I showed the slightest sign of disobedience he used to lose patience. 'I don't know what ails her,' he said. 'I recollect when I was a boy I'd have had a good hiding for that.' He turned on Mother accusingly. 'I reckon she must have got the "botts",' he said. 'Well,' Mother replied, 'if she have I know who she take like.' Then off they would go in a fierce argument, my misdeeds quite forgotten.

By the time I was five years old the little school in Lacton had closed down and a governess was hired to teach me at home. No government official ever checked on the education of what Mother called 'better class people'. Only the working classes were hounded to school, so my illiteracy went unremarked. Mother found a governess convenient so that was the end of the matter. She was another maiden lady of uncertain age, wearing long skirts and a velvet neck band. It was she who told me that no lady is ever older than twenty-nine, so I suppose she remained that age for ever. She was a thin lady, with a scraggy neck which folded over the band at her throat, and her faded ginger hair was drawn up into a big bun on top of her head. She was very refined but she could not teach me to read. Lessons were in the mornings only. Every mid-morning there came a knock on the door of the wireless room, where I was imprisoned. On being permitted to open the door I found a tray with two glasses, a big jug of home-made lemonade and a doily-clad plate of tiny delicious sandwiches standing in the hall. We stopped lessons to partake of this feast. Never, never was I allowed to eat the last sandwich. It had to remain on the plate and be carried out of the room again because, my governess insisted, we must always leave one for manners. Daily we did battle over that last wretched sandwich, but she always won.

As my sisters were out at school all day, and no other children came to share my lessons, I was left in a vacuum without competition in work or play. My governess did her best to make up for this by telling me about her niece Betty. I do not know if Betty really existed or if she was invented for my benefit. I was told that she lived in Harpenden and it seemed that she never put a foot wrong in her life. Whatever I did, she did better or else she did not do it at all because it was unladylike. Everything she did was ladylike. I never stopped hearing her praises and I hated her. Apparently no one ever thought that I might need the company of other children of my own age. None were forthcoming beyond the ghostly Betty until I went to the convent at the age of eight. It is not surprising that I cried: school terrified me.

Although Father was against all formal school education, nevertheless there were three things he thought we ought to learn: to row a boat, to drive a nail and to cut bread. He required us to cut the bread quite straight, using a saw-edged knife, and not to make a single crumb. After each slice Father gathered up the offending crumbs and, holding them out in the palm of his hand for all to see, said, 'Try again, and this time keep your wrist down.' He got more and more exasperated as we went down the loaf. 'Drop your wrist, I tell you!' he shouted. Being a miller he always had a plentiful supply of test loaves for us to practice on. Milly managed well enough and I enjoyed it because it was satisfying when you began to get the knack and could make your hands work correctly, but for Skinny it was her Waterloo. She began to cry, knowing that Mother would come and rescue her from her tormentor. She hoped that there might be a row, with Mother and Father getting

so angry that they forgot the bread-cutting entirely. Skinny's tactics incensed Father. 'The mauther's leary!' he shouted. 'She wants to be certified!' Secretly, Milly and I agreed with him.

Rowing lessons took place on Sunday afternoons. A little grey punt was kept on the river, as well as an ancient rowing boat, tied up to the garden steps, and sometimes Father decided to take us all out on the river. One Sunday we had been a long way up the river and were getting rather bored and fidgety on the return trip. Father was rowing himself and he expected Mother to steer and the rest of us to sit still and keep the boat trimmed. Suddenly he lost patience with us and shouted out to Milly, 'Why the hell can't you keep your arse in the middle of the boat?' At that moment we rounded a sharp bend in the river and came to face to face with Father's solicitor, who was fishing from the bank. I shall never forget Father's discomfort, nor our delight. Solicitors were people for whom Father thought it necessary to use his best manners and 'talk Trevor Page', and he hated getting caught out.

Mother was nervous in a boat and she created a great fuss when Father made us all stand up and change places if he wanted a different one to row. He thought a certain amount of nervousness was becoming in a wife so he did not object to Mother's fears being voiced. Very occasionally we persuaded Mother to take us out in the boat when Father was not there. We children never went by ourselves; it was absolutely forbidden. Mother could handle the boat very well and was so proud of her daring that, in the evening, when Father came home she could not resist telling him, 'I took the girls on the river this afternoon.' At that Father frowned. 'You want to mind none of you don't duzzy in,' he replied balefully. It was a good thing the boat never capsized. Father could not swim at all, and Mother could only manage a few strokes in a tentative way, keeping well within her depth. Milly once told a schoolfriend, 'My Mother swims with one foot on her bottom': a contortion she was never allowed to forget. Milly seemed to learn to row quite easily, but Skinny made hard work of it, and cried and declared she could never do it. 'Now my lady,' Father told her, 'don't you start putting on your parts with me!' When he said 'my lady' it meant he was getting angry, and we always took it as a signal to be careful not to provoke him further. I came off best in the boat because I was too small to manage both the heavy oars and had to take one, with Father at the other. I could never keep time with him. In exasperation he used to seize my oar as well as his own and pull with me. I watched his beautiful brown hand with the very long, strong fingers resting beside mine on the wooden oar handle. Father was very proud of his hands and their immense strength. Once, when really angry after an argument with Mother about a newly-acquired cottage in the village, he took hold of the garden railings, two in one hand, and squeezed them together just to vent his rage. That showed everybody what he could do, and I was most impressed, but I remember seeing Mother turn and walk away without saying a word. After a moment of deathly silence Father walked off in the opposite direction, leaving me standing beside the bent iron outside the cottage.

Although he thought all females were fools with money, Father was determined to knock as much sense into us as he could. He found it uphill work. He was sure that some luckless men would turn up and marry my sisters for their money, which had been left to them in Grand-dad's will, and of which Father deeply disapproved. He really worried about it, and was constantly warning us against gold-digging suitors. When Skinny and Milly were old enough for boyfriends, none appeared, so Father was proved wrong and he did not like it one bit. He tried to persuade Mother to take the girls on a holiday with a big party of millers' families, run by an organisation of which he was a member. He thought it might result in them meeting and marrying suitable millers' sons whom he could later take into the business. I overheard this being discussed and Mother's haughty refusal to go. At the time I was disappointed because I wanted to go and vaguely thought Father was right and that a wedding would be fun. It never crossed my mind that they might have gone without me, though looking back I realise how little my sisters would have wanted me to play gooseberry if they had found any boyfriends.

Within limits, and as long as he was certain to win in the long run, Father believed in bringing up his daughters to question authority and show a bit of spirit. We got our pocket money not each week but monthly to encourage us to husband our resources. It was considered our place to ask for the money; Father never offered it. If I went to him on the last day of the month to ask for mine, Father said it was too soon and refused to pay me. If, next time, I went on the first day of the new month, he said I was too late. I was expected to stand my ground and fight for what I wanted. If I did that I always got it. On one occasion I was sent across to the mill office to cash a cheque for Father. When I got back and presented him with a handful of notes he counted them and said the bundle was one pound short. He told me to count the money myself, and on doing so I found that he was quite right, one pound note was missing. Had I counted it in the office when I took it from the clerk, Father asked. No, I had not. Father raised hell. He said it was all my fault and I ought to pay the pound out of my pocket money. At last, when he had nagged long enough, he slid a pound note from under his bottom. He had slipped it down the side of his chair and been sitting on it all the time to see what I would do. 'Let that be a lesson to you!' he said. 'You always want to count money when anyone give it to you.'

It was just as well that Father was a natural optimist: in the face of his eldest daughter's school career he needed to be one. Skinny managed to achieve one long series of failures for which she could not be blamed. She fainted in exams when she was old enough to benefit from such tactics and she always supplied some good reason for Mother to be sorry for her and to fly to her defence. Milly was, by comparison, clever at lessons, and it soon became accepted in the family that she was the clever one and would end up a schoolteacher. Mother found this most satisfactory. Whenever we got into trouble together she said to me, 'You never thought of that. Milly put you up to it.' This always riled me because usually I had thought of my fair share of the mischief, and even of some of the worst things we did, and I felt I had every right to get the credit and the punishment, but Mother had cast me in the role of her innocent baby, and that was the end of it.

Milly was often ill as a girl, and Mother and Dr Rodwell decided that sea air would be good for her, so after a while she was taken away from the convent and sent to a boarding school on the coast. This was a tremendous event and one which held so much glamour that Milly enjoyed it right from the start. The school was a tiny place in North Norfolk run by two maiden ladies of uncertain age. Dressed in shapeless frocks and long beads, with sensible shoes and their grey hair cut short and neat, they were everybody's idea of 'blue-stockings'. They were very academic ladies. Father did not enjoy meeting them, but Mother did. She revelled in their book-lined study. When they could manage it, my parents used to take Milly back to school in Father's huge old Daimler. 'We're sure to have a puncture. We always bloody well do on that road,' Father declared, as he made the car ready for the journey and packed in his passengers. Any trip over fifty miles seemed an adventure and a driver was lucky if he could get that far without a puncture on the tyres and road surfaces of those days. If the Daimler did not get a puncture on the outward trip it always had one on the way back. It was useless to expect anything else.

At school Milly pleased Father by winning prizes. He went to all our school speech days in his best suit and sat waiting to hear our names called and see us get our prizes. That was what he went for and it was up to his daughters to keep winning. Skinny was a failure, and I proved regrettably unreliable, but Milly's school career was the success which Father expected. If we did not get a prize, or worse still failed an examination, he blamed Mother entirely. After all, she was the champion of women's education so she was responsible for seeing that his daughters came out well and did him proper credit. 'If the buggers are going to be educated then they might as well make a decent job of it,' he said, but in spite of all Mother's and Father's efforts there remained some very big gaps in my knowledge, and music was a total blank.

No one could have called my parents musical. Mother liked to listen to talks on the wireless, but when the programme changed to music she always said, 'Put that old row off.' Nevertheless she loved playing her piano and sometimes sang hymns as she played them. Father could persuade her to play songs too, but not very often. He wanted to join in and get the rest of us singing with him, although we were the most tuneless lot imaginable. When Uncle Bernie came to stay he used to start the singing. 'Come on Gracie,' he said, 'play "The Mermaid".' Then Mother had to thump out "Rule Britannia" and he sang, 'Britons never, never, never shall be mar-ri-ed to a mer-mi-ed at the bottom of the deep blue sea!' Father's special song was, 'I wish I was single again, Oh, I wish I was single again! When I was single my pockets did jingle, I wish I was single again!' He accompanied himself by jingling the coins in his pockets to drive the point home, and he tapped and stamped his feet too. Mother never played for that song. She sat looking down her nose until Father was quiet, but she could not stop him grinning about it. Another of Father's songs which she appeared to dislike even more was, 'Oh, Mother, I long to be mar-ri-ed, I long to be a bride. I long to have a good man to lie down by my side. For Mother, you very well know, I'm of the woman kind, and it's such a pity a girl so pretty as I should lay alone.' We never heard the second verse because Mother always said, 'Stop that low old song!' and Father did. He had to provide his own accompaniment to that song too, but it did not put him off at all. He held up his trouser legs and capered about. It was a fine way to irritate Mother.

Father had his own song which he had made up himself, and which needed no help from a piano. When I was very small I would climb on his knee to be bounced up and down as he sang,

'Hipperty, jipperty, jopperty, jo,
Hoary, moary, poary,
Hikey, mikey, pikey, crikey,
Hullabawillabagory!'

118

It was the best song I ever heard. Mother sang all the songs of her Edwardian girlhood, with the result that those are the songs which I know best today. As she went round making beds and doing household jobs she sang all the time. 'Oh let the *prairie* echo, God bless the Prince of Wales!' always puzzled me. I preferred, 'Ta-ra-ra boom de-ay, The Duke of Clarence's gone away, He's gone to heaven, so they say, to sing ta-ra-ra boom de-ay.' Another song we all sang was 'Clementine'.

'Light she was, and like a fairy
And her shoes were number nine,
Herring boxes without topsies
Sandals were for Clementine.'

and the last verse,

'Now at night she always haunts me
Clothed in garments soaked in brine.
Though in life I used to kiss her
Now in death I draw the line.'

I have never been able to discover whether these verses were in current usage or if they were a family improvisation.

When Mother played the piano she was lost to the world, and we found that she would say yes to any request we made rather than stop her playing to listen to us properly. After we had used this to our own advantage enough times, Mother got wise to it. Then if ever we said to her, 'But you promised we could do it,' she would counter with the dreaded question, 'Was I playing the piano when you asked me?' If we were forced to admit that she had been, then she declared that her promise was invalid, and we had to look for a different way to 'get round her'. Although to please Father and Uncle Bernie Mother could play songs, for her own pleasure she chose hymns. Her favourite, 'Abide with me,' she sang with great pathos. Perhaps she did feel the darkness deepening sometimes, having such a family to deal with. Another hymn I remember her playing was, 'Forever with the Lord, Amen, so let it be!' Father bought her a Salvation Army hymn book so that she could play,

'Dare to be Daniel,
Dare to stand alone,
Dare to hold to your belief
And dare to make it known!'

He approved of that one, the only hymn he would sing while Mother was playing.

On the rare Sundays when we went into the drawing room Father liked to play the gramophone. The first record he chose was always Harry Lauder singing, 'Keep right on to the end of the road,' and he usually joined in and sang too, tapping his feet to the music. Father told us we could each choose a record to be played. Milly got her favourite easily enough, 'The Road to the Isles'. The rest of us thought it excruciatingly funny because to us the Scots accent was quite unintelligible, and we used to wait for the end of each verse and then sing loudly, 'You've never smelt the candle or the oil.' Indeed we always referred to the record by that name, but we did not succeed in discouraging Milly. Before I could get a chance to say what I wanted, Father always chose for me, 'Who killed Cock Robin?' It terrified me, it haunted me, and it lasted over two sides of the record so that I used to pray that something would happen, or that tea time would come to prevent us hearing the second side. I am sure that no one knew that I loathed it; I sat through it with my face stiff, smiling when I ought to smile and never letting on how I felt. In those days cheerful family teasing was considered the cure for any peculiarity or foolish fear. It did you good to be laughed at, everyone said, and they proceeded to taunt you, trying to get you to lose your temper. Merciless family jokes were made to last for months, and repeated over and over again. The victim's only defence was to maintain an appearance of tight-lipped indifference to all tormentors. If the teasers got no reaction they got no fun, so they gave up in disgust. Putting up with endless teasing was supposed to be a useful lesson in self-control, which would come in handy in adult life, but what a small compensation this offered for so much misery!

At Christmas singing played an important part in the festivities of the village. Groups of children came to sing carols under our windows. Mother kept a pile of small change in the hall, ready to hand out at the end of each performance. She opened the front door wide to see how many children there were and to identify each one if she could. She peered out into the darkness and if she noticed a familiar face skulking at the back of the group she said accusingly, 'You've been before! You were here last night!' Then the offender would not be given any share of the evening's hand-out. Mother really had to take a firm stand on this or there would have been no end to carols, and to the coppers and sixpences she doled out. It was not unusual for as many as four or five groups of singers to come one after another each evening during the week before Christmas. The door would hardly close on one lot of children before the next lot of singers started up.

Sometimes Mother played carols on the piano at Christmas time, and Father, hearing her begin to sing as she played, would leave his newspaper and come down the hall to stand in the drawing room doorway and sing too. He sang his own schoolboy versions of most of the carols.

He liked,

'While shepherds washed their socks by night,
All seated round the tub,
A bar of Sunlight soap fell down
And they began to scrub.'

Much to Mother's disgust, I soon learned Father's words to the carols. However her disapproval was only very mild, as religion, after all, was best not taken too seriously. One great favourite of Father's was,

'Hark the herald angels sing
Beechams pills are just the thing.
Peace on earth and mercy mild,
Two for a man and one for a child.'

That always made Father and me laugh.

Being a life-long member of the WI and a vice-president for a lot of years at the village branch, Mother took part in their community singing. In the days before I was sent to school I was taken along to the practice sessions, and had to sit at the back and keep quiet. Mother could not leave me with my governess because that lady was a WI

121

member too. Miss Emily Randall took charge of the singing and conducted the assembled ladies with a long pink knitting-needle. Practice was held in the front room at 'The Laurels' and I was the only person present who was not required to wear a hat. Instead I was forced to put on clean white socks for the occasion. Hats for ladies were all but compulsory then, and Mother often complained of the discomfort of keeping hers on during tea parties. Sometimes ladies who came to tea with Mother, if they were old acquaintances, would, with great daring, say to her, 'Do you mind if we take off our hats?' and Mother said of course she did not mind, whereat the ladies started wrestling with their hat pins, and let out great sighs of relief as the hats come off; but they always waited to see who else was coming to tea before they flouted convention. If anyone of importance in village society was present the hats stayed firmly in place on the ladies' heads. Miss Emily was never seen without her hat, and it did not move an inch during her ladylike sweeps with the pink knitting-needle. They sang, 'Oh, no John! no John! no John! no!' and 'Soldier, soldier, will you marry me, with your musket, fife and drum?' Sometimes they attempted 'London Bridge is burning down', sung as a round, but this was usually a disaster and ended with Miss Emily trying to quell the arguments of the singers and to calm the ladies down again. I do not remember hearing them sing 'Jerusalem'. Perhaps it was not the WI song at that date, or perhaps they simply knew when they were beaten.

In the country districts the only entertainment was the wireless, so the village relied heavily on concerts, plays and whist drives 'got up' in the school or the Hut, to give a little zest to life. There was no cinema nearer than Norwich then, let alone one opening on Sundays. Mother expected us children to take part, as she did herself, in all the village's attempts at entertainment. She felt bound to take a lead in getting things going. Poor Skinny was made to dress up and dance a sailor's hornpipe in the Hut. There was no stage, but an empty space was left at one end for the performers and the piano. Skinny, wearing a sailor collar and a brave attempt at a sailor hat, with a navy blue blouse and skirt conveniently provided by her school uniform, circled round the floor, prancing to the tinkling music, occasionally thumping back on her heels as she mimed pulling on an imaginary rope. The unfortunate girl also had to do a dance which Mother was firmly convinced was an Irish jig. The Irish connection was established by providing Skinny with two squares of bright green silk. One square was tied securely to the little finger on each of her hands so that she could wave the silk about without fear of dropping it whilst she danced.

Milly and I were not much good at that kind of thing. Milly was too clumsy, and I was too young, Mother decided. The only time I ever performed at the Hut was when Mother was organising the entertainment, and I was put into a kind of 'action song'. For this, Mother, Milly, Skinny and I were lined up facing the audience. I had to start. I took one step forward and chanted,

> *'All you good people who take Grape Nuts*
> *And give your neighbours none,*
> *You shall have none of my Grape Nuts*
> *When your Grape Nuts are done!'*

That was all I had to do, indeed it was all I could be trusted to remember, but as well as being the shortest piece, it was also the first in our act and Mother was terribly worried that I might be afraid to begin alone and the whole thing turn out to be a failure. I managed my verse, and when I had finished, Skinny, who stood next to me, sang,

> *'All you good people who take Ipecacuana wine,*
> *And give your neighbours none,*
> *You shall have none of my Ipecacuana wine*
> *When your Ipecacuana wine is done!'*

Milly was taller than Skinny so she stood between Skinny and Mother. Milly's verse began

> *'All you good people who take Oxo what killed my poor brother*
> *And give your neighbours none ...'*

On the word 'killed' she crossed her eyes horribly, and did so again each time she repeated it. She did it superbly, and the audience was entranced. They laughed so much that Mother could hardly be heard when she finished the act with,

123

'All you good people who take Dr William's Pink Pills for Pale People ...'

It was a great success, or at any rate we thought it was.

Father would never have dreamt of attending a village concert. He let the women get on with that. Certainly the audiences were largely composed of women. It was understand- able that they were ready to enjoy the most trivial of amateur shows. Domestic work was all that was available in the village. A few girls went to the 'Works' in Lacton, but not after they got married. Only those married women desperate for money went out to do housework or took in sewing or washing. Normally they remained at home, struggling to bring up their families, and apart from a good gossip there was not much fun to be had. Father got his gossip at the markets and he appeared not to feel the need of fun or entertainments; nevertheless, wherever we went he always wanted to hear all about it when we got home again, and usually we gave him a detailed account. 'Now I know as much as them what went,' he declared comfortably, having heard us out. Mother was infuriated. 'He always try to get the know out of you,' she said. 'Why don't he go himself? I won't tell him nothing the next time!' But by the next time she had forgotten her resolution and was easily enticed into telling Father all he wanted to hear.

Father did not give much thought to pleasure for himself. He was totally absorbed in running his business and making a success of it. Although the mill was his pride and joy, his first love, nevertheless the responsibilities of family life weighed upon him heavily. He had always worked hard and was satisfied that he had done his best for us, in spite of his disappointment that we were all girls. Watching, as I began to grow up, Father realised that I might have to face a hard world beyond the shelter of home, and he could not conceal a prickle of anxiety. 'I suppose,' he asked me, 'none of them at school don't never say anything to you for being only a miller's daughter?' I was able to assure him that they never did.